Corporate Coach Approach

Corporate Coach Approach

A Systematic Guide to Career Development

NICOLE FRONEK

Published by Painted Gate Publishing

Copyright © 2024 by Nicole Fronek

All rights reserved. Content within this book may not be reproduced without written, signed, and dated advance approval from the author. Brief citation in other publications, or references made in reviews are permissible with appropriate citation adhering to industry standards.

The opinions and professional recommendations expressed in this book are that of the author. This book is not endorsed, nor sponsored, or in any way the property of companies the author has worked for, of current employment, or consultancy services under contractual obligation, excluding Two Horse Productions LLC of which the author is the CEO and co-founder thereof. Two Horse Productions, LLC, located in the Black Hills of South Dakota, serves as a source of original content and consultancy services, inclusive of, but not limited to career advancement and professional development.

Books published in association with Two Horse Productions, LLC are also available for bulk purchase to advance professional or educational development. Visit www.twohorseproductions.com for more information.

ISBN # 978-1-952465-57-4 (Paperback)
ISBN # 978-1-952465-58-1 (eBook)

Edited by Vitus Sinkovits
Book design by Nicole Fronek
Art direction by Vitus Sinkovits & Nicole Fronek
Cover art by Danial James

Published by Painted Gate Publishing
Printed in the United States of America
First Printing June 2025

In loving memory of my late father who demonstrated the power of question without criticism and heartfelt praise for any achievement, large or small.

CONTENTS

Foreword	2
Introduction	4
1 – Personal Branding	8
2 – Resumes 101	19
3 – Write Like a Journalist	30
4 – Stakeholder Engagement	41
5 – Nobody Cares	54
6 – Meetings and Conference Calls	65
7 – Presentations	78
8 – Take Action	89
9 – Corporate Environments	100
10 – Performance Reviews	112
Conclusion	124
Appendices	127
Appendix I	Key Concepts	128
Appendix II	Acronym List	133
Acknowledgments	135
References	136
Index	148
About the Author	152

FOREWORD

Stepping into the role of Executive Director, there were more questions and doubts than confidence. While deeply committed to the organizational mission, leadership, especially the kind that involved public speaking, group training, and high-stakes decision making, felt daunting. I needed a seasoned mentor who understood the nuances of executive communication and could teach me to lead with knowledge and present. That mentor was Nicole Fronek.

Nicole is more than a coach. She is a motivator and a master at helping people uncover strengths they didn't know they had. Through her guidance, I learned to present ideas clearly and, more importantly, to believe in the power behind my voice. What once was intimidating, leading meetings, facilitating trainings, and standing in front of an audience, has become one of the most energizing aspects of my work. That transformation didn't happen overnight. It came through strategic, thoughtful coaching sessions, shaped by Nicole's knowledge, ability to turn complex ideas into practical tools, and unwavering belief that growth is always possible.

Nicole helped me develop more than skills – she helped me shape a leadership identity rooted in compassion. Her mentorship laid the foundation for what would later become the heart of my personal leadership philosophy: Empowered Advocacy. That clarity and confidence were spared through the coaching techniques described in this book.

What you hold in your hands is more than a guide. "Corporate Coach Approach" is a blueprint for professional development for anyone who feels like they're still figuring it out. Nicole's voice on the page is exactly how she is in person: direct, insightful, funny, and practical. She cuts through the noise to offer real world strategies – whether you're polishing your resume, leading a team meeting, or navigating complex workplace dynamics.

The book is a testament to Nicole's years of experience across corporate environments, her gift of professional communication, and her unique ability to coach individuals toward confident, effective leadership. Every chapter leads to one powerful truth: you don't have to fake confidence – you can build it. And when you do, you don't just perform better at work, you show up differently in every area of your life. Nicole's coaching has made a measurement difference in my professional growth and personal outlook. If you let this book guide you, it will do the same for you.

- *Heidi L. Mecham, Executive Director*
  Workplace Disability Network of the Black Hills

INTRODUCTION

"Excellence is the gradual result of always striving to do better." - Pat Riley

Passion, according to Merriam-Webster, is defined as a "devotion to some activity, object, or concept". I am passionate about career growth and the unexpected ways that development occurs when open to new ideas, or in response to a change in course. Improvement not only applies to processes and procedures, but is also applicable to individual performance. Year-over-year, or YoY in corporate shorthand, a pattern of requests from family, friends, and colleagues fell into categories such as, resume enhancement, presentation opinion, and career path assessment. As my exposure across various Fortune 500 environments increased, so did requests for coaching. In parallel, I found myself as a source of reassurance for those confronted with challenging clients or disorganized initiatives. Enthusiasm placed into perfecting an email or meeting agenda, activities typically deemed as mundane, transformed opinions of my process from rigid to highly effective.

An ability to edit quickly, or arrive at a reasonable solution with limited data, I forged an expected quality within my inner circle - 'The Coach' label was cast in stone. Dozens of recommendations were shared with those interested in development. Feedback indicated that publications were complex or did not resonate to the present employment landscape. Inquiries for something new, while cutting to the chase, became too frequent to ignore. Learning the hard way, observed by many as an exercise in patience, deemed inefficient. Such traditional methods, akin to earning your stripes, are no longer practical. Employers demand prompt results, attempting to do more with less, where advice seekers want answers. Experts in the field of occupational coaching are numerous, yet a single source of consolidated expertise, similar to what was routinely shared across my network, lacked. In the pursuit of seeking what could not be found, the '*Corporate Coach Approach*' materialized.

Chapters one, two, and three form the groundwork in establishing a professional identity. The application of branding is no longer reserved for large conglomerates, but instrumental for individual representation. Resumes, serving as supportive documentation, should emphasize qualities, distinctly yours. Communication proficiency is necessary, whereby integrating journalism techniques is worth consideration. Four through seven explore building relationships and driving productivity throughout day-today engagement. Meeting and conference calls, numerous and broad in subject matter, consume schedules, demanding participation on various levels. Whether lead or guest, perspectives gained from years of trial and error are compressed into a high-level overview discussing both scenarios. Lastly, eight, nine, and ten focus on action and accountability within a corporate setting. Even when serving as a part of a team, monitoring self-performance is critical to maintain personal aspirations. Advocating for ones' growth is as important as striving to achieve organizational objectives.

In short, this book offers an extensive range of knowledge, curated over time, in a summarized manner. Each topic includes an evaluation of situations encountered and concludes with a checklist reinforcing key concepts. The structure offers a quick and informative view into the 'best of the best practices' in areas repeatedly asked about while offering insights on integrating technology, namely features associated with AI (Artificial Intelligence) platforms. Theme selection, therefore, based on a passion for growth expressed by others. Pause for a moment to determine what you are passionate about and why you were drawn to this publication. Whether the aim is to increase confidence, maximize advancement opportunities, or retool an established career, treat content as 'all-purpose' for a range of industries and skill levels. While a cover-to-cover reading is encouraged, content is designed to offer immediate value regardless of order. As such, review in its entirety, or jump to a subject of relevance, gaining insight when it matters most – the moment it's needed.

CHAPTER 1 | PERSONAL BRANDING

"If you're not branding yourself, you can be sure others do it for you". – Unknown

Similar in concept to a reputation, a personal brand is representative of the way others perceive you. Lending clarity to how the two differ, Monarth (2022) describes reputations as built from opinions formed from "behaviors" whereas a personal brand is about "values that you outwardly represent" with purpose. Further simplified, reputations are inherited, whereas brands are intentional. In my experience, reputations develop when actions are observed in response to roles and responsibilities assigned. Branding on the other hand is guided. From this context, consider the value in playing a significant role in distinguishing yourself from peers. I've come across many colleagues who misinterpret the influence of self-branding; their attitude towards branding along the lines of 'a nice idea if there was time'. Deprioritizing branding activities is a grave disservice in career development; the very act of dismissal behavior becoming a part of their brand. The time avoiding branding would be better spent shaping an image reflective of positive visibility. Therefore, personal branding should be a priority as it is the foundation of an individual's identity.

An opportunity presented itself while supporting a national manufacturing company specializing in corporate branding. Following the office closure of our Midwest division, my boss arrived deskside with a stack of cardboard boxes. The words that followed seared into memory, "you are the only one in our department that is organized enough to figure this out and save the account". I was seen as middle-management at the time, and leadership's interpretation of my brand did not come as a surprise. I was routinely voluntold for complex situations of this type - an opinion or a reply not expected, nor needed, and therefore, not given. Due to the urgency, a resolution strategy was required in 24-hours. I would, however, receive a dedicated resource for administrative support over the next month. Two team members would barely be enough for this particular undertaking - requesting one was in my best interest given the limited resources. As such, careful brand assessment of those available was a strategic play. The next morning, the coordinator selected arrived with a notepad and pen in one hand, and a coffee for me in the other. I had chosen wisely.

This program was a classic case of poor performance. Over budget, behind schedule, and incorrectly built products destined for the scrap pile. The previous team reported false information to headquarters for six months.

Compounding the issue, the flawed data was presented to the client as well, resulting in a five-hour initial call with the primary stakeholder. Painstakingly, I sat in front of a sea of falsified documentation and took the heat for the sake of the company. Digging into the true picture of program health, as terribly over schedule and budget as it was, a revised report, offering a dashboard-like overview, was created and distributed. Approximately two months in, client-based meetings were lessened to once a week. Files stacked at my desk at the onset, now ready to be retired to the shredder. I built an extraordinary relationship with the client and gained an entire portfolio of work in the process. Expectations exceeded; brand qualities known for were further solidified. Within the quarter, I was promoted to team lead and two smaller accounts reassigned allowing additional focus on client development.

In contrast to the above scenario, repercussions when veering from an expected quality level was observed while employed as a project coordinator. An improvement consultant was hired to identify and streamline processes within the manufacturing division. Across from a row of small, oddly wallpapered offices, a large warehouse stood 25 feet tall. The metal enclosure was filled with every noise imaginable. Bells, buzzers, and rattling resonated from aisles of machinery. Each Thursday afternoon, like clockwork, the consultant assembled the department leads and asked the same questions. Although the group entertained this tactic for four months, eventually cooperation ended. The consultant looked around the room and arrived at my gaze. Apparently, I was the most willing to speak as everyone else conveyed a 'don't think about it' stance expressed through folded arms (never underestimate the power of body language). Unscripted and brutally honest, I expressed that the consultant could not ask the same questions and expect change. Time would be better served on the production floor. The consultant disagreed and another month in front of a diagram congested white board ensued while raw material waste and overtime accumulated. The CEO told the consultant not to return.

Each initiative being unique requires in depth evaluation of relative complexities. A similar line of questioning asked in repetition is ineffective; when solving problems, creativity is necessary. Both the executive consultant and I were placed into assignments by leadership due to our proven track records, however approaches differed. While the same tools and methods could be utilized from one scenario to the next, my questions are specific to the matter at hand, not generalized. I firmly believe the executive consultant knew this premise to be true as well, but gave in to complacency, resting on previous success. The act of such is not uncommon and can jeopardize a favorable brand positioning. When reputations validate expectations, integrity is retained as the intended prescription of brand is clearly understood. When actions do not match with expectations, credibility is lost.

With the above in mind, consider how others may finish the following statements:

- I hear you're great at ....
- I admire your ability to...
- The way you managed that event was impressive because ...

If conclusions to the above phrases were easily identified, an image is either well-established or tracking in a positive direction. Conversely, if completing the above comments proves challenging, a clear brand is undefined; a scenario when a career is in the initial phase and contributions are too few to form an accurate opinion. Either way, be mindful that impressions begin when prospective employers review resume submissions (Chapter 2), thus long before an interview occurs. From recorded voicemail greetings to email correspondence, do not leave perceptions to the imagination of the audience. Preferred messaging should resonate throughout all content, digital platforms included, representative of abilities and aspirations, (Weiss, 2018). Once a brand is defined, routine monitoring is a best practice to preserve integrity.

All instances of exposure and participation affect brand recognition. Consider skills that you find easy, but are deemed taxing by others. These proficiencies identified are 'superpowers' – assets in Corporate America. Once isolated, hone positive traits for continued improvement. In parallel, brand familiarity forms a benchmark as to what is expected from individuals. I've experienced that when seen as having a natural ability to lead, requests to manage an initiative, or lend a hand in client relations, is common as crises surface. If a company is trending towards a negative standing, the overarching corporate brand is on the line as well. Being singled out from your peers to act in a position of leadership, especially in complex situations, is a true testament of confidence in abilities.

A well-rounded understanding of an image guides choices and actions (Wright, 2023). As those with authority deem coworkers with proven brands as trustworthy, additional consideration of inclusion for special projects may trend upward. When, where, and to what extent you will be asked to help, and able to do so effectively, will vary. To self-determine availability, evaluate standing commitments, development goals, and the needs of the team if managing direct reports. Proactive workload forecast assessment places you ahead of the curve of most; having the foresight to plan ahead necessitates discipline and is indicative of a self-starter. Stephen Covey, internationally recognized for his profound teachings on professional growth, promotes being known as a strategic thinker, rather than a people pleaser (2020, p. 208). Ad hoc, or as needed, involvement, beyond existing obligations, requires a careful balance of time management and assessment of available resources. Conversely, taking on more responsibilities through volunteering with the intent to enjoy the recognition, but delegate the work is a poor decision. Some falsely believe this is smarter, not harder practice is acceptable; however, the approach is a surefire way to damage a brand. If you are hesitant that taking on one more item will risk optimal service levels associated with, do not raise your hand.

As fully remote and hybrid roles increase across various industries, in-person face time diminishes. Focused attention directed at strengthening relationships during events, like all-hands meetings or corporate conferences, is essential. Treat professional relationships with genuine consideration for how impressions impact brand formation. A potential avenue to gain visibility where a remote setting is typical, is volunteering. Special assignments enable organizations to facilitate client scalability, or improve processes for cost reduction measures. Each offering opportunities to earn recognition or acquire skills outside of a role assigned. Associated activities provide pathways to reinforce credibility, or generate awareness for your brand across a broader audience base. Others' comfort level, also known as trust factor, is critical for career progression. Coleman regards exposure as the pinnacle to advancement, valuing visibility (60%), above image or perceived brand (30%), and performance (10%). These percentages challenge the classic saying of 'it's not what, but who you know'; rather, it is who knows you and to what extent.

In agreement with Colemans' assertions on visibility combined with differentiation, Arruda and Dixson (2009) cite the need to generate "career distinction" centered on qualifications that only you offer. Proficiencies of each individual are uniquely theirs; as such, replication is not possible, and therefore not a strategy to pursue. Standing out in a crowd taking on new meaning as engagement is largely trending to a digital presence. Cyberspace leaders, a group more elusive than ever, are no longer confined to marble-clad offices and walls of paneled glass. Where the majority of tasks blend into the background, chance encounters with those of power and prestige must be impactful. These are the 'money' moments of visibility. For those who seek elevated roles within their organization, demonstrating a "digital-ready" capacity is advisable (ManpowerGroup, 2023, p. 7). Meaning, does your brand showcase the ability to inspire and guide remote teams? Do strong face-to-face strengths translate to a screen capturing the attention of stakeholders and colleagues? In short, would you be effective in project delivery if in a 'digital space'?

To that end, whether a brand is forming or developed, integrating technological competencies is a necessity. Digital dexterity, or the ability to leverage and adapt to technology inroads, exhibits an understanding that change is evitable (Abelli, 2021). When seeking new employment or internal opportunities, consider that the market sector or role itself is not as important as how the perception of your brand is received (Ford, 2021). Therefore, it is crucial to maintain branding authentically yours. As appropriate, identify ways to add value to the organization. Don't know where to start on a task? Enter a prompt into a chatbot for suggestions. Continue seeking digital advice until confidence is achieved. From that point, apply elements from your unique experiences and personal style. Content recommendations from chatbots and other AI features should be treated as just that – recommendations. Validate that messaging conveys what is intended, and is reflective of preferred traits.

Consideration of brand management in all that you do is highly beneficial as affirmed by Monarth (2022) remarking that it does not matter how great you are at your job if your individuality is unknown. Fundamentals such as a positive demeanor and reliability are key elements of brand association and should remain in focus regardless of physical location. Along with traditional offices, hybrid or Work From Home (WFH) settings are increasingly common. Remote workspaces necessitate that branding efforts receive "daily deliberate action" (Arruda, 2022) to remain "relevant in this new environment". While in-person meetings, conferences, and training have reemerged, the volume has declined, reducing opportunities for the physical act of shaking hands. That being the case, it is increasingly important to meet with colleagues where possible. Engage with your team often and with purpose. Be resourceful and help others solve problems through integration of technological advancements. Branding does not need to be set in stone, but should remain authentic.

CHAPTER 1 | BEST PRACTICES

1. Craft a brand with intention and monitor to preserve its integrity.
2. Every engagement is an opportunity to solidify preferred perception and increase brand familiarity.
3. Reflect on in-demand skills that are inherent; market these superpowers as assets.
4. Adhere to core values as it pertains to ethics and trust; integrity matters.
5. Form an identity synonymous with a leader - forge a path, do not follow blindly.
6. Success often materializes from helping others perform at their best. Demonstrate team-centric behaviors in daily activities as you forge relationships.
7. Remember, there is always room for improvement; accepting constructive criticism expresses maturity and professionalism.
8. Evaluate workload routinely ensuring quality levels are sustainable to complete existing commitment and before volunteering.
9. Suggested chatbot results should act as a starting point. Edit and refine AI generated content to reflect an established brand.
10. Digital environments contribute to image; take advantage of opportunities where applicable and do not become complacent.

CHAPTER 2 | RESUMES 101

"The simpler you say it, the more eloquent it is." - August Wilson

A resume or CV (curriculum vitae as widely utilized in European countries) describes an individuals' background in a professional capacity and at face value is a seemingly simple document. However, when confronted with a blank page, or standardized template, the exercise of summarizing a work history is more challenging than most anticipate. As a result, repetitive content fills multiple pages, emphasized by exhaustive bullet points. On occasion a bit of flare is inserted by way of objective statements or list of hobbies. If any of this sounds familiar, you may be rolling your eyes recalling the countless times your resume has been revised, revamped, or dropped into the recycle bin. Oftentimes, individuals struggle with deciphering value-add contributions from routine responsibilities. Unless you are a rocket scientist or applying for a position in academia, a single page document is sufficient and as such, is a big undertaking. In addition to being impactful, and intriguing, Gannett (2018) denotes that a resume needs to be grammatically correct and typo free to avoid appearing careless. Effective resumes are concise, informative, and relevant to the role you are applying for; this structure forming a winning trifecta.

One week after accepting a role post undergrad studies, I received an in-depth compliment specific to resume structure. My supervisor had hired dozens of employees throughout their career, but ultimately was impressed by the amount of data I was able to compress into one page. Descriptions of support were sophisticated and the overall presentation clean. Unable to put a finger on the exact word at first, the compliment evolved into a conversation until an epiphany materialized - the document was well organized. I was not only extremely flattered, but proud. Arriving at the optimal blend of information and stylistic formatting had been a labor of professional love for a good many years. A former classmate, a Senior Human Resources Director today, was even enlisted to review what I believed was a final draft; the input in return deemed invaluable given the volume of submissions seen routinely. With only two minor adjustments, confidence in my appraisal was solidified. The assessment of my peer further validated when asked by my manager if my resume could be shared with other job seekers as an example of a quality document – personal identification information redacted. I was slowly growing into 'The Coach' designation that would follow two years later.

My early resume attempts were far from eliciting any amount of admiration. Applications were sent to any and every employment posting that presented itself. I needed an adult job, because I needed an adult salary - desperation must have been apparent. To sum up the sharp pains of defeat felt long ago, hiring managers were not certain what exactly I did, or could do, in connection to the job I applied for. Constructive feedback was ultimately that I read postings more carefully to reduce wasting their time and mine. A painful wakeup call as not only was I unqualified for the vast majority of roles, resume reviewers could not get a sense as to whether or not I was a good fit for the organization. Line after line of exhaustive explanations lacked data demonstrating growth from one company to the next. Stakeholder understanding was marginal, proven in wordy expressions too flowery to make heads or tails of what value could be derived from my contribution.

As it relates to documenting experience, the challenge for an individual early in their career is the exact opposite of a seasoned veteran. Those new to the talent pool do not have enough experience for a full page and must resort to flourish and creative wordsmithing. To the contrary, the established professional must be frugal with depictions of background, editing layer upon layer of experience to zero in on substantial examples of success. The difficulty surfacing from too much work experience is deciding what noteworthy elements should remain as to differentiate from an unknown number of qualified applicants. Accomplishments that generated significant merit, or cost saving measures for the company are best to broadcast, but with precision. Did you develop a business unit from the ground up creating an additional revenue stream? Did you save an account by isolating and resolving a quality concern? Think of yourself as a product or service offering and the possibilities of your contribution if given the chance.

Quarterly Business Reports, or QBRs, are documents generated in corporate settings to showcase previous quarter productivity. As a best practice, update your working resume in parallel to key milestones such as QBRs. The benefit is that details are current and fresh in your mind. Maintaining an up-to-date document as a routine habit, mitigates the need to retrace specifics at a later date. If the most recent file in your computer includes a multi-year gap in employment history, consider your weekend gone, spending hours recalling information during the time-lapse. Secondly, if asked for a resume by a manager, or prospective employer, providing immediately demonstrates a highly organized and motivated individual; a powerful combination of attributes that shapes or preserves intended branding (Chapter 1).

Strengths should not be 'told' through listings of related responsibilities, but shown through condensed summaries of achievement. Resumes providing qualitative and quantitative data lend evidence of measurable results, otherwise referred to as a proven track record. Entries accounting various positions held ideally include numerical validation as well as the quantity of locations, projects, or the like, managed or monitored. Inform the reader through specific values, which is favored over dense descriptions (Weiss, 2018). In agreement, Heath and Starr (2022, p. 37) emphasize that concrete values, rather than abstract details, increase comprehension and the speed thereof. Software or processes utilized to indicate how a task, or initiative, was executed through completion is also important to denote in each bullet point. This formula showcases role complexity and responsibilities adding credibility of contribution. Read each line out loud to catch grammatical errors and to check for ease of comprehension. Edit, then read again. If a line of text is difficult to speak or understand, delete it and move to the next; one page will fill quickly and space is valuable.

Opposed to what *should* be added, a few thoughts on what to *avoid*. Any words or phrases that may elicit a negative connotation, should be repackaged to indicate a solution-based approach taken to reach a resolution. For instance, consider the phrase of how you 'dealt' with an item, rather than how you resolved or developed a solution. Word choice can express a certain undesirable 'tone' that could be perceived unintentionally. Arruda *et al.* (2009) advocate for describing how "solutions to challenges" were identified and resolved. Bullet points in the experience section, therefore, serve as an opportunity to highlight added value in corrective measures to generate positive outcomes. In corporate environments (Chapter 9) direct line supervisors consider overall chemistry, and if your personality type would complement that of the teams'. While a first assessment is made when a resume is reviewed, opinions are solidified during the live interview process.

You may be thinking that your social media presence, combined with a well-constructed digital portfolio should be enough, or a reasonable substitute for a resume; surely, better than one page, right? Wrong. Resumes are, and have been a mainstay of the business world for centuries. While the first record of utilization is attributed to Leonard De Vinci, the current practice of advertising professional experience drew from technological advancements of Microsoft products such as Word©, and IBM hardware (Burdick, 2017), increasing the efficiency of resume creation. Digital profiles posted across online portfolios and personal websites could set you apart from multiple qualified candidates, however, upholding traditional standards is a good best practice. Regardless of what software is utilized to create the document, soft copies should be saved into a PDF format before distribution to preserve formatting.

Almost on a monthly cadence, I am asked to review a resume. The reason is that attributes associated with my brand (Chapter 1) include proficiency in reconstructing content for improved flow. Self-editing is difficult as 'everything is equally important' in the mind of the creator. Despite how wildly accomplished you were at the last gig, success must relate to the prospective company's needs; otherwise, 'that's nice, but of no use here - delete'. Adequately condensing an entire professional career into one page, while validating cultural fit, is equivalent to nailing an interview. Input from another point of view is beneficial for clarification, interest, and general readability. Everyone interprets material differently; something obvious to the author may not translate as well as expected. An outside perspective is recommended as a final form of checks and balances.

Job offers alone are reasons to celebrate – added attention garnered by the structure or brevity of your resume, truly humbling. Just as skill development occurs through exposure, effectively communicating capabilities in written form is a craft that improves from time at task. When building your document, do so from a historian-minded perspective. Once employment and academic sections are drafted and areas of expertise listed, review from the lens of an editor. Would it be clearly understood what the candidate (you in this instance) excels in? Does the career path objective stated align with the position? Along with what you are able to include, consider programs, certifications, and potential deficiencies you may need to invest time towards in order to revitalize marketability. Be patient, and do not feel pressured to rush through the exercise of resume development and perfecting as opportunities are explored.

Two centuries ago, 70 percent of the American workforce lived on a farm (Dormehl, 2017); this way of life was altered by the "capitalization effect" which automated a range of jobs previously performed by manual labor. Fast forward to the present, digital tools and services have flipped the script on traditional methods of seeking employment – history repeating evident. Data being the "new oil" (Ford, 2021), highlights a digital dexterity will serve you well once in a role, however such traits may be necessary to land a job in the first place. Customizing a search to your field of interest may arrive at the perfect match, but standing out to receive an interview invitation remains another hurdle. As such, there are those who are concerned with retaining a role and others who find it nearly impossible to secure a job as resumes flood inboxes for the same opening. A significant factor is that in the not too distant past, candidate hopefuls were put off by creating yet another cover letter, or modifying a resume to include role-specific keywords. Yesterday's attitude of "I'll pass – it's not worth the hassle" resolved by AI solutioning - a few clicks and submissions tailored to align experience to need. The sea of candidates is increasing by and large given the ease of applying. Continuous development to align with "evolving demands" of organizations (Grady, 2024), more important than ever.

Ongoing career contingency planning compensates for the unknown and increases agility in response when market disruptions occur, or technology evolves. AI and the impacts thereof present another dimension of corporate environment consideration and retooling of competences businesses may include as a prerequisite to securing employment. Some will be challenged with traditional career mapping and finding their place as new to market roles form in support of Metaverse virtual space evolution, Chief Metaverse Officer for example, a role in its infancy at present Hackl (2023). With the ushering in of added complexities to the contemporary workforce, organizational success requires creative innovations, as well as technical proficiencies. A tall order for candidate hopefuls - the ambitious need only apply.

RECOMMENDED FORMAT

1. Contact information – place at top: name, address, email, phone number
2. Career accomplishments – significant contribution, 2 to 3 lines
3. Technical aptitude - certifications relevant to the role and unique to your skillset
4. Experience - 10-years maximum; include school or community exposure as necessary should you be junior in your career.
5. Professional affiliation - entities relevant to the role or that align with a brand.
6. Education – Entity name, location, year, degree type, and major/discipline
7. Embedded Footer - include full name and date of resume version.

CHAPTER 2 | BEST PRACTICES

1. Brevity! Consolidate as possible, such as with software suites opposed to listing each item included within.
2. Format should be easy on the eye; use a standard font and 1-inch margins.
3. Show NOT tell. Include values, durations, and the method/tool utilized to achieve accomplishments described.
4. Language and tone representative of your preferred branding (if in-development) or in alignment with expectations (where a brand is established).
5. Read out loud. If something sounds 'off', it often is.
6. Complete a spell check and grammar review, twice. Yes, again!
7. Save the file with a naming convention inclusive of your full name and a date. When sending, or uploading, the document should be in PDF format.
8. Do not go it alone. Research digital resume builder tools to select the best fit.
9. Ask someone to review the final draft; fresh eyes may find items overlooked by the author due to familiarity or isolate an error in computer generated content.
10. Do NOT include 'References available upon request'; this phrase is an out-of-date practice. Many companies conduct background checks or expect references are possible to furnish otherwise.

CHAPTER 3 | WRITE LIKE A JOURNALIST

"The most valuable of all talents is that of never using two words when one will do." - Thomas Jefferson

Constructing an informative and intriguing narrative, while maintaining brevity, is not an easy feat. Word choice, structure, tone, and cadence are all critical elements contributing to clarity. To keep pace with meeting schedules and daily obligations, skimming emails and documentation is, at times, necessary. The use of familiar language and well-arranged content is advisable to achieve "processing fluency", otherwise referred to general comprehension (Birchard, 2021). Writing competency, however, is not an attribute one possesses, but is classified as a "correctable skill" (McKloskey, 2019). Therefore, seeking proven methods in message conveyance is a worthwhile goal. Entire bodies of work dedicated to this theme are widely accessible; ranging from workshops to online training material, composition proficiency can be treated as a mainstay of personal development. Improvement through repetition is achievable, or in the words of famed Fahrenheit 451 author Ray Bradbury (2012), "quantity produces quality".

Shifting from interior design to project management involved a broad shift in the way I approached tasks. Relying on strengths associated with organization and customer service served me well at the onset, but fell short at times. In an initial project management-based role as a project coordinator, layers of detail resulted in unintentionally complex emails. My logic was that if answers to anticipated questions were included, the audience could make well-informed decisions - I was wrong. Routinely, the reader would reply asking what was needed of them, or request a call for clarification. While well-crafted, the conclusion I arrived at was that messaging was too elaborate and exhaustive for daily engagement. Meaning was lost in the act of decoding required on the part of the receiver. When possible and without much risk to their own role or responsibility, my emails were filed into oblivion or deleted. I know this to be true (colleagues told me). If important enough, others just assumed a meeting request would follow – a fair assessment.

In 2007, I began a new role for a fledgling company. Just shy of the infamous two-year mark start-up firms dread before being deemed out of the woods, financially speaking, the economy took yet another turn and the next week, unemployment became a reality. While focused on increased marketability during an uncertain time, continuing education felt like a viable solution. Weighing options, a communications program was recommended by the student career advisor. Coursework included the prerequisite of Journalism 101, which caught my attention. Challenged by the professor in week one, we were to write as if each word had a monetary value. Instantly astounded, I began to examine communications as if I was an editor. Within the first month of experimental messaging in the workplace, productivity increased. Responses were prompt and questions were answered at a higher volume than before. Before the end of the semester, my manager was heavily repurposing emails I composed for their own correspondence. An act bordered on plagiarism, but I took it as a compliment. From that semester on, writing less was no longer a goal, but a standard. My signature brand, in written format, solidified.

There is no way to know what my career would look like today had I not opted to reconsider my educational background. I knew I was at an impasse in professional advancement as my skills did not translate as well as expected outside of the commercial design sector. With a decade of experience, I was no longer classified as an entry-level employee, however the change of industry required a step back for a leap forward. With sights set on exploring project management, or PjM, for the long-term, retooling my academic career towards communications was a logical choice as the profession of PjM is centric to engagement with others - as high as 90 percent (Haus, 2016). Essentially, activities associated with communication can form the majority of a day, inclusive of email correspondence, conference calls (Chapter 6), presentations (Chapter 7), and status update tracking. An ever-evolving art, the ability to communicate effectively is a valid objective for individual development.

The act of looking to specialists in an area where you'd like to improve is not a groundbreaking concept; yet we may find ourselves guilty of overlooking the obvious on occasion. Inclusion of the five W's and H (who, what, when, where, why, and how) forms the core of journalist writing. A formula found to be efficient, this standard is utilized in various methodologies such as Six Sigma, an iterative process focused on continuous improvement (Mahalik, 2010). These descriptive elements convey pertinent details in interpersonal communication, such as origin, context, and level of involvement to anticipate. Along with formality, style or tone, effective messaging takes shape. An additional factor is providing sufficient context. Information void of adequate background detail, or vague requirements, can hinder comprehension and can potentially incur a delayed response. Arguably, there is much to bear in mind concerning everyday correspondence; leaning on the expertise accumulated by others is a logical method.

Clarity of expectations is essential to achieve results. For example, when delegating a task, timelines and next steps should be concise. Adjusting the font of due dates to bold and coloring in red is not out of line, rather appreciated as to attract attention. Indicate the 'why' behind the importance of the task. A novel is not necessary, however background details for added context often increases the quality of feedback. The two key factors of 'when' and 'why' allow tailored responses improving understanding for the action item. Second-hand tasks, assignments subject to layers of delegation, are prone to be lost in translation. If the original message clearly defines objectives, there is a better chance that the task or request will be understood and fulfilled. Also, providing the full picture in correspondence for non-routine, or particularly pressing matters, increases the likelihood that others outside the original audience will be able to associate with the purpose, and lend additional support to the best of their ability.

An online presence should not be overlooked when accounting for how messaging may impact a broader group of readers. Prior to the wide adoption of the internet, the printed word was the pillar of community outreach. Each letter produced by the press, formed by ink, incurred an actual cost for inclusion. According to Bagadiya (2023), Facebook users alone log more than one billion posts daily. While Singh (2022) denotes that each post consists of 13 words on average. If each word were to cost you one US dollar, how often would you post a comment on social media? Or if deemed important enough to share, how much shorter could the posting be? A few workshop-style exercises for practice follow:

Writing Less: Evaluate a recent email or social media post. Reflect on the intent or action expected in return. After some thought, determine what sentences could be eliminated without risking comprehension. Oftentimes, reversing the order of words allows elimination of an 'of' or 'the'. Automatic application of such techniques takes time, but is worth the return on investment (ROI).

Pronoun Usage: Some favor heavy pronoun usage, subconsciously or unintentionally, as to make a point. The mighty 'I' is associated with power or authority. Ironically, high-ranking executives strategically omit 'I' from correspondence, opting for 'we' or 'our' to create a collaborative environment (Bashaw, 2019). Pronouns at a minimum offer a secondary benefit of refined content. Review former emails and look for frequency of pronoun use. If the volume is high, attempt to reduce going forward.

Duplication: Avoid overuse of words and phrases to mitigate the perception of lazy writing. Repetition bores readers and diminishes credibility of subject matter expertise. Before clicking 'print' or 'send', perform a 'search/find' to replace duplications that are close in proximity. This act isolates redundancy in word/phrase combinations that may go unnoticed otherwise.

Self-Edit: Conducting a final edit as a standing protocol is essential to ensure flow and accuracy in grammar. Reading out loud is a technique to confirm sentence structure is as expected. If something is difficult to say, it is all but certain it will be hard to understand. My standing rule when it comes to final self-editing is that if a sentence or phrase does not flow well after three attempts in adjusting, it's deleted in full. Either I am uncertain what I want to say, or it does not need to be said. The point was already made or is not relevant to the overall message.

The work entitled *Economical Writing* by McKloskey (2019) caught my attention recently as I reflected back on the guidance received years prior in journalism class. The profound impact of one college course set the principle of cost-effective writing into motion. I find that such a class is not on the radar for many unless there is a direct connection to the field of study. Without the program core requirement for journalism, this topic would not have been an obvious choice among a list of electives. Another point promoting building knowledge of standard journalism methods is that you find yourself in a position of being interviewed by a journalist at some point in a career (Branson, 2012). For these reasons, I highly advocate to all who request professional coaching recommendations to enroll in a journalism course, or workshop at minimum, irrespective of role, industry, or age. As my college professor alluded to years ago, writing is a process enhanced by practice.

When utilizing AI-based resources, specific questions or instructions, a process known as 'prompt engineering', will provide a more robust result. Dormehl (2017) emphasizes that including wording into a prompt statement, such as "AND, OR, and NOT" indicates clear direction of what should be included or omitted. By this logic, integration of journalist techniques into daily business writing follows the same foundational principle. For a firm understanding of intent, or to gain/maintain interest of those on the receiving side, descriptive statements should include as many relevant elements (5 W's and H) as possible. Lacking components of significant value, such as when a task is due by, can lead to confusion of expectations from the audience. With this in mind, the realization that use of AI tools for written communications offers an ability to enhance, not replace, original concepts (Newman, 2023). Content still being your own, just elevated in quality (clarity) or brevity (length). From this perspective, it is necessary for the creator (you) to possess an ability to write well (effectively to get your point across) in order to benefit further from AI integration.

Communicating well does not necessarily mean communicating more. Writing less requires patience, persistence, and discipline. When implementing the idea of associating a monetary cost to your writing, intentional word selection slowly becomes habitual and subsequently, less strenuous. Regardless of role, industry, or authority, a baseline of communication abilities is expected by the hiring entity. Many employers assert the desire for exceptional written proficiency, but settle for good to fair out of necessity. From solidifying favorable perception, to increased speed of results, catering messaging to those on the receiving end, often creates a sense that you understand needs and are fully able to execute stated commitments. Working to achieve superior levels of correspondence is not an aspiration of many in the corporate world from what I have seen. In my opinion this is unfortunate as it can trigger a domino effect of positive outcomes. Focused detail on comprehensive messaging, followed by strict editing, is a surefire way to set yourself apart from peers.

CHAPTER 3 | BEST PRACTICES

1. Write economically as if each word had a monetary value.
2. Include 'who, what, when, where, why and how (The 5 W's and H).
3. Add visual punctuation (bold, underline, coloration) to highlight important needs, but do so sparingly as to maintain intended impact.
4. Review final drafts to determine if a sentence can be deleted; often repetition occurs without realization. Where comments are not duplicated, but relatable, combined with a semicolon.
5. Be strategic with pronoun usage; include when essential for emphasis or comprehension.
6. Avoid repetitive verbiage; keep a running log of favored words/phrases, and perform a 'search/find' in while editing.
7. Strive for clarity over complexity to alleviate confusion. Sophisticated vocabulary is not recommended for daily business communication - save it for the academic world.
8. Seek opportunities to write for a variety of audiences for diverse perspectives.
9. Use content generating tools as a sort of writing coaching enhancing your concepts and business-driven narratives – still you, just better.
10. Be patient with developing effective writing skills; this trait is not natural, but an intentional choice.

CHAPTER 4 | STAKEHOLDER ENGAGEMENT

"Strive not to be a success, but rather to be of value."
– Albert Einstein

As the saying goes, if you do not like the weather, wait a few minutes and it will change. Similar in corporate settings, no situation is permanent. Organizational procedures evolve, divisional leaders transfer, and consumer markets ebb and flow to name a few examples. An attitude towards how a circumstance is approached, however, can be the one variable that is possible to regulate. Reframing the concept of relationship management, positive perceptions of professional interaction is a category for career betterment all its own. In the workplace, daily engagement occurs between individuals of varying levels of authority and responsibility. Such participants, referred to as stakeholders, have a vested interest or direct bearing on outcomes (Vogwell, 2003); the extent being dependent upon their level of influence and authority. Simply put, organizational success is contingent on how well colleagues collaborate.

Only minutes before a business development call with a new client, I was asked by the host to reschedule due to a conflict. Instead, I offered to maintain the meeting, inquire of any immediate needs, and secure a good time to reconnect. In agreement with the proposal, I signed into the call to find a screen filled with camera ready attendees. With a warm and calm tone, the proposal suggested to the host moments ago was shared, with details of why rescheduling was necessary purposely omitted on my side (Chapter 5). I paused to scan facial expressions. The representative of the client facing team questioned and commented simultaneously as to how I transformed an inconvenient schedule conflict into a strategic planning session with such ease. Composure sets the stage for productive interaction, or in some cases, alters the overall dynamics mitigating an otherwise challenging scenario. From various experiences, addressing items calmly has become a branding style default. This example captures a brief moment in a standard workweek, yet reveals how positive impacts can occur long after a singular event. In calls with the same group thereafter, the established rapport from what could have been a missed opportunity, shaped into a collaborative stakeholder relationship.

In severe contrast, I've witnessed rapid dissolvement of a once united front. A business unit of a large corporation was contracted to bring a new system and service model online. The stakeholders, quite literally those directly impacted by the changes, were slowly, and intentionally, removed from critical integration discussions as to avoid questions leadership was unable to answer. It was not until the day before the switch was flipped, that the affected department was informed of the extent of imminent changes. Management expected that staff would adapt because they were told they must. Integrating a new workflow with limited input gave rise to upheaval and unsurprisingly – catastrophe. With no time to familiarize themselves, trial by fire became the only option. Effective stakeholder engagement was made impossible for those responsible for, ironically, stakeholder engagement. Earlier conversations treated as confidential amongst a select few, incapable of understanding the implications of disregarding client relationship best practices, backfired. Department reputation shattered; meager results were deemed unacceptable compared to costs incurred - a complete 180 from where the group began, a true business upset.

An ability to bring others together in a meaningful way is an honorable attribute to strive for. My development call, turned workshop described at the top of this chapter, demonstrates unexpected value from stakeholder engagement. Message acceptance, rejection, or disregard may offer clues into the perception others have of you.

How you react can strengthen or weaken an existing affiliation, or form a new alliance. In short, the chemistry of a group is unpredictable. Some colleagues are risk takers, others risk averse – Go/No Go decisions often arrive at a stalemate when personality types differ greatly. Repercussions of ignoring impacted stakeholders can ultimately come to a head and likely create an irreversible, adversarial environment. Assume the role of a stakeholder broker (Herman, 2021, p.234) to guide respective sides vying for their position to reach a mutual understanding. In doing so, development of an invaluable skill set can emerge where creative and diplomatic strategies merge, for the sake of progress.

Anticipated involvement of a stakeholder can be calculated by organizational standing and authority level. Both elements influence outcomes, but many factors come into play. For instance, consider stakeholder management, a premise based on defending a position challenged by opposition (Kujala, Sachs, Leinonen, Heikkinen, and Laude, 2022). Protecting one's team, division, or objectives at all costs, is a predictable tactic to avoid risk of unfavorable conclusions. It is not uncommon for negative impressions to form outside of our control – guilty by association when in a group setting. Not all colleagues will take stakeholder influence as seriously as they should. (Recall the dissolved department example shared – the overarching team brand adversely altered by actions of a smaller subset). Positive associations of the way in which interaction occurs is critical to career advancement; that being the case, where possible, choose your corporate allies wisely.

The term engagement has gained traction in organizational settings, redirecting cross-functional participation away from the idea of managing individuals. Consider that individuals who are senior in their positions, rose through the ranks by conducting business in the methodology of the past - traditional, tried and true methods of familiarity. It is tough to change course when proven track records extend a sense of security; new strategies that are yet to be tested lack credibility and adoption can lag as a repercussion (Kessler, 2018). From this idea, execute tasks from the position of an ally, not a competitor or an anchor. Be gracious to those who offer support in return, but do not dismiss clues in messaging or body language that they themselves are uncertain or overwhelmed.

Along the same lines, some disregard their own limits and press on in spite of the fact that they may not be in the right frame of mind to process additional input. As a result, irritation, poor decisions, or speaking out of line could induce resentment among colleagues. Jack Welch, the famed CEO of General Electric (GE) has been quoted, cited, and studied by many authors and corporations. Rather than a particular phrase, I offer a consolidation of concepts described in 'Get Better or Get Beaten' (2001) concerning the power an individual has to drive change, bring value to an organization, and influence productivity-rich environments. This combination aptly conveys an idyllic mindset in business concerning stakeholder engagement. Interaction, when at your best, can remarkably improve outcomes. Proven by science, peak performance is associated with chronotype mapping, or the window of time where work quality is optimum, generating high quality output (Pink, 2018). Following suit, acknowledging the ideal time of day for others is worth consideration as to extract the best in return.

Observing when attention spans are at their limit seems to be a dying art in the digital landscape. It is surprising how unaware some are, ignoring body language, or worse yet, actual comments verbally expressed. Based on verbal and non-verbal signals, determine if it is best to wrap up the conversation until a later date, or possibly readdress with a different party at another juncture. Also, it is not unusual that the original group is no longer as impactful or relevant as when efforts began. This situation can stem from changes in roles, interest levels, or business objectives of the company. If a significant adjustment in audience is needed to adapt to altered conditions such as these, create a new forum to realign expectations with the new audience. Consider perspectives of the individuals now present to learn from previous contributions. As inconvenient as feedback may feel at the time it is received, it can be a valuable source of information to plan next steps for effective engagement of those impacted going forward.

A 'can do, everything is my job' stance can catapult favorable opinions of an individual's work ethic or level of dedication. Not to stray from a personal brand (Chapter 1), or biting off more than you can chew, nonetheless ambition is admirable. Being too eager to lend a hand, can lead to chaotic or unreasonable demands within a standard workweek. In cases such as these, create a priority tracker where the amount of time anticipated is clearly indicated along with a brief description of the task. It is normal for a stakeholder to lose track of what has been requested. A well organized and simple 'to do' list provides visibility of all requests to date while showcasing an interest for overall success. Supporting various stakeholders in parallel requires maintaining existing commitments at sustainable levels. Working together accommodating conflicting obligations is a reasonable approach to isolate solutions in workload management.

Impressing colleagues, managers, and clients is difficult enough in person, let alone virtually. Building a rapport with peers and clients through a digital persona is a reality many will face. Based on statistics, from 2025 onward, over 32 million Americans, or "22% of the workforce" will work from home (Haan, 2023). While some desire a remote role, that does not necessarily mean they will thrive in one. Remote roles romanticized in mass, visualize the traveling blogger or columnist, sitting in a lounge chair, laptop perched open. While deep in thought gazing out into the snow-capped peaks, an award-winning story comes to mind in an instant. How did the Wi-Fi connection reach that far from the building? I ruined the moment; however, this plot twist is a wake-up call you may thank me for at a later date. While a retreat-like work environment is achievable, you'll have to come down from the mountain eventually and answer to someone. The good news is that from my experience, how stakeholders view you is dependent on their level of comfort and established trust. Are you considered reliable and proficient to the degree necessary to aid advancement of their career? To this end, it is worth emphasizing the point that in certain instances, your assistance might be a variable in someone's ability to be promoted or mitigate job loss. While important to remember in the corporate setting, it's business, not personal, there are appropriate ways to *personalize* matters that pertain to professional settings.

As companies seek to benefit from AI integration, the act of role consolidation may be viewed as a logical cost reduction measure. Employees known to provide a level of superior customer care through relationship management are not all together immune from reduced headcount, however the likelihood of an extended tenure in their current position may be in their favor. The reason being that successful interpersonal skills remain in demand as these traits are not yet possible to replicate through automation at comparable levels (Ford, 2021). Qualities such as creativity and empathy are predicated on human interaction – a viable digital substitution not yet in place for utilization (Tasaka, 2020). Machine learning is ever growing, yet innate skills are difficult to transcribe into a formula or program. The result is that a machines' ability to support a client in totality remains a lagging component of automation-based tools.

Organizations who seek to find success in maintaining client care needs with automation may move the needle, but should keep in mind that cognitive competencies are still critical in times of emergency management or when confronted with a distressed client. Mimicking, or a system's ability to build upon added input received from data entry, can improve recommendations in reply to problems described through prompts (Fearn, 2024); but complex decisioning requires a level of sophistication contingent upon human contribution. The practice of "hyper-reflection" is described by Madsbjerg (2023) as analyzing the background, for added depth beyond what is obvious. The ability to engage in effective communications is the top ranking "power skill" across all industries as reported by the Annual PMI Global Survey on Project Management survey (PMI, p. 10). Interpersonal skills, therefore remain highly relevant.

Organized individuals often regarded as keen observers are classified as having a balanced disposition. An ability to perform a role, in an environment where innate talents are recognized and routinely called upon is gratifying. The added luxury of time and space to create from a proactive mindset - nirvana. When fully present and confident, a person can facilitate dialogue or mediate differences to shape quality relationship management. I find that candid criticism increases as individuals feel heard. Creating opportunities to speak freely amongst a group is a coveted attribute to strive for, a careful balance as not to stray away from constructive conversation to office gossip. As colleagues, or clients, gain comfort, bonds are built, and productivity increases. Therein significant progress materializes. Before engaging in another conversation with a colleague, manager, or client, consider how to build trust, remove barriers, and generate environments where objectives are attainable.

CHAPTER 4 | BEST PRACTICES

1. Stakeholder credibility is often gained from resolving a problem; be known as a solution provider and barrier remover.
2. Where feasible, coordinate engagement when you can be at your best - time of day, conflicting priorities in obligations, or physical location are key elements to consider when undivided attention is necessary.
3. Invoke genuine buy-in by creating opportunities for mutual perspectives as more is discovered about personalities and preferences of those you work with and for.
4. Understand the goal before providing options, opinion, or commentary.
5. Request visibility to a shared calendar - 'view only' at a minimum, for those supported routinely. Managing expectations includes consideration of availability – avoiding requests for engagement (where possible) during lunch, late afternoons, early Mondays or late on Friday (Chapter 6).
6. Professional chemistry cannot be fabricated - it exists or it does not. When possible, consider alternatives to investing energy in a forced partnership that is unlikely to become a valuable relationship. Examples include:

   - *Request a different representative if the contact is an external vendor.*
   - *Seek another role in the group that limits interaction of low to no value.*
   - *Enlist the support of a proxy or alternative point of contact.*

7. Remember the notion of 'it's business, not personal'. Lean on policies and procedures to counter stalemates and arrive at agreeable resolutions.
8. Remain humble when recognized for a job well done – such moments are worth celebrating, but are often fleeting. Do not grow accustomed to praise.
9. Like a computer, never stop learning. Utilize digital solutions to further refine skills specific to your personal brand (Chapter 1).
10. Seek ways to help others look good and thrive in their role. Constructive dialogue when challenges are shared can shift vulnerability to a sense of solidarity.

CHAPTER 5 | NOBODY CARES

"*Nobody cares, work harder*" - John Gretton "Jocko" Willink Jr.

The proverbial phrase 'there's always one' is a concept describing how a collective is adversely impacted from a single source. Inaction or interference can disrupt an otherwise balanced situation. The previous call ran over, unaware of the double mute option, software updates not possible to postpone – the plain truth is that simply, nobody cares. Inspiration for this chapter, therefore, is based on a spectrum of characters you'll encounter at some point, and sadly, repeatedly. In short, disrupters to productivity come in many forms. Either making a scene to garner attention, or forming an excuse to distract from assigned tasks, these employees become the aggravator, the interrupter, the irritant. From experiences with such classic examples of a bad apple, such a reputation is typically self-inflicted. Often subjected to that one individual who arrives at the scene, contributes nothing of value, then leaves a puzzle to untangle after being fired or asked to resign. Left with only a disaster as a reminder, the entire episode was all for naught. While offering a bit of mid-book amusement, practical tips and revealing antidotes of patterns to watch for help determine where to conserve energy, and who to monitor that may be working to derail productivity.

When this chapter was under development, I took a late lunch break to get some fresh air. On the way to the table, a t-shirt of a fellow patron caught my eye. It read, 'Nobody cares – work harder'. My belief in the value this chapter could bring was validated in an instant. Not in the gray, no walking on eggshells, this article of clothing provided affirmation, quite literally in black and white. Following this fortuitous dining experience, I did a search on the message displayed on the t-shirt. To my surprise, dozens of hits surfaced, ranging in messaging offering inspiration to be better, train harder, or give it your all. Upon further research, it appears the saying is associated with authors Willink and Babin (2015) from the context of military excellence through leading with accountability. From the premise of professional interaction in the corporate world, simply performing a role, to the best of one's ability, is possible without scores of unnecessary, off-topic information.

Someone boasting of technical expertise, yet repeatedly not having the ability to execute the share screen feature with success, or consistently plagued by audio problems, is baffling. Without exaggeration, there was a year-long period where one individual began every call with a string of comments as to why they were late - the culprit being their own equipment. Contrary to the statement made at the onset of participation, meetings ended with an overly confident message that their computer proficiency was gained from their time helping teammates and external vendors. Without correction, their manager allowed this behavior, month-over-month, or MoM, without regard for the costs incurred in the form of lost productivity. With an average of six calls a week, a captive audience of up to ten were subjected to an inconsistent self-defeating 'I can't because' statement, concluding with 'I always help others because I am so capable" declaration. To tie a bow on this story, I'll conclude with a bit of satire. When employee X was relieved of their position, everyone cared - a shared relief, inclusive of the external vendors that had been 'helped' over the past year.

Business etiquette is a straightforward concept, yet disregarded unconsciously by those who display behavior most in need of change. Whether this statement is believed to be cynical or harsh, it is a reality. After years sitting at a desk, supporting industries and clientele of a wide variety, I have yet to observe an environment free from useless information broadcasted without regard for the jam-packed schedule of others. Household pets in a brawl in the living room causing plugs to be pulled from their socket or landscaping equipment, at deafening 100 decibel levels, right on cue when a critical project update is needed. Such occurrences, irrelevant to the topic at hand, become quite convenient and welcome distractions. Then as if enough time was not lost waiting for the interference to subside, how pet names were arrived at brings story time full circle. People who took care of interruptions, on mute without a spotlight, will certainly be aggravated. While a one-off oddity could offer a bit of comic relief, insert sparingly, and where suitable.

In every organization a few select individuals fall into a classification of attention seekers. These usual suspects are always late, talking on mute, or plagued with a technology glitch. Their participation upon arrival exudes stress and is curiously repetitious. Initial support, or an emphatic, friendly face, will fade in time due to exhaustion and frustration. Attendees who made it to their workstation, after rushing through the kitchen, spilling their coffee or tea, will be enraged to witness that their timely dial-in was pointless. 'So-and-so' true to form, is unable to hear anything, but remains motivated to deliver a five-minute monologue of the trials and tribulations of the steps taken to adjust headsets and microphones. Not pausing for a breath until gaining a thumbs' up emoji. Everyone else who did not have issues joining the call, will promptly turn off their camera, roll their eyes, and re-engage with a different activity to feel some sort of accomplishment opposed to sitting idle.

After identifying those who fit such a mold, it begs the question – could these tactics be premeditated acts to avoid work or discourage involvement in group projects? Could these people really struggle with adapting to basic software similar to that of a smartphone, or systems used daily? In actuality, such ploys are staged to detract from either a lack of fundamental skills vital to their role, or a deep seeded confidence issue. In either case, the behavior displayed is not witty, charming, or clever. A delicate balance of how to help the weakest link eventually turns into quick dismissal as conveniently timed inabilities continue to manifest themselves. Their time to respond to a project deadline oddly occurs at the moment of signing for a package. Or, better yet, the battery power of a phone or computer in the red - 'oh shame, I forgot my charger'. Yes, of course, things of this nature happen. Yet, is it plausible that items of this sort happen once a week, or worse – during every meeting? Try again as no one will believe this to be the case.

Origins of the statement 'less is more' stem from an 1885 poem (Browning, line 78). However, Ludwig Mies van der Rohe, the German engineer, architect, and furniture designer, popularized this catch phrase with his enduring quest to enhance design through simplification, all the while improving functionality and aesthetics. Treating occurrences of professional engagement from this perspective helps monitor verbal excess. I've found that the airing of dirty laundry has become increasingly prevalent in the digital environment. It is as if everyone has managed to feel comfortable, or inclined to overshare. A feeling of security from behind the screen perhaps provides a false sense of importance or is repurposed as an opportunity to hide in plain sight. Mistaking the captive audience as genuine interest could be the root cause. Those on the line are earning a wage in exchange for participation. Rest assured; the primary goal of attendance is not to learn about the rigors of a morning commute. Repurposing a meeting for a therapy session, to lament shortcomings, is poor form and can tarnish a personal brand.

'Mute all' is the digital indicator that nobody cares. When facilitating calls, be bold, save the company money and spare employees who are punctual and prepared. Preserving the agenda and allotted time, requires confidence and specific messaging. Inform the audience that to remain on schedule, while allowing a caller an opportunity to reset or readjust, the line will be muted. Submitting a grievance for the application of this feature requires effort and follow through; activities that non-producers despise. As an experiment when hosting a conference call, observe camera utilization when agendas veer off course. Those ready to engage, but stifled to do so as others are rambling on about nothing will tune out and potentially, log off. Producers produce - it is in their DNA. Therefore, if an environment is not conducive to productivity, it is repurposed. A proficient host is equipped with the good sense to recognize colleagues of this variety and shapes a platform for thoughtful engagement. Allow these individuals an opportunity to provide a status update, then fade into the background to accomplish tasks or drop from the line altogether.

From countless hours supporting startups and Fortune 100 firms, I have developed a new appreciation for K-12 educators. Excuses such as contagious rashes, upset stomachs from spoiled food, or pets destroying documents, all in hopes to avoid a poor review, have spread like wildfire through the workplace. Have we, the workforce, allowed this behavior simply by being kind enough to listen? Permitting minutes to pass before extinguishing obvious deviations from the planned conversation could be seen as a form of complicity or being confrontation-averse. In either case, the potential consequences of calling someone out, is being labeled as rude, dismissive, or unsympathetic. Redirecting dialogue is uncomfortable in some instances, but necessary if professionalism is questionable, or falling into a downward spiral. If unclear how best to handle the situation, simply state that moving on is for the sake of the time allotted. If you hear someone indicate that the matter needs to be taken offline, it is highly likely someone is treading on thin ice. A delicate balance is necessary to be considered effective, yet compassionate. As such, mindfulness of tone and attitude offers a logical approach in facilitating difficult calls. Adequate preparation for meetings, and forming an alliance with peers who work tirelessly to offer the same courtesy in return, is honorable.

When in an unfamiliar setting or new role, the best way to acclimate is to dive right in. Not sure where to start, or how to initially address an issue is no longer subjected to laborious trial and error. As AI-supported functionality increases, independent study opportunities are limited only by imagination and ambition. From summaries to detailed reports, information on any topic is accessible around the clock. Utilizing digital technologies as an on-demand tutor eliminates flying solo when seeking ways to resolve a particular challenge, or obtain specifics in a knowledge area of which familiarity lacks. Submit a detailed prompt into a chatbot browser, and in mere seconds, recommendations flood into view for review and consideration. This being the case, colleagues that ask questions related to routine topics, or how to troubleshoot a common hardware issue, could signal a few things. While the act possibly stems from being uncomfortable with chatbot automation (AI interaction), more likely the case is that the individual is lazy or unable to break a nervous habit of self-disclosure. Regardless of why, daily encounters layered with 'Chapter 5' elements are irritating and burdensome. Repeated excuses call after call will not go ignored for long. Much like being a house guest, try not to wear out your welcome allowing coworkers to retain their energy for quality client engagement.

Attention and intention are key principles to understand where participation is of quality opposed to quantity, and how small adjustments during engagement add up. It is not realistic to avoid all disruption, and not all disruption is meant to derail an initiative. As each person in an organization is responsible for their contribution, preserving energy for the sake of the quality input needed from you is a reasonable stance. To remain accountable, establish and maintain your limits. Join required calls - for example those requested of your boss requiring your attendance specifically; however, where some leeway allows, choose wisely. While you are typically unable to avoid 'employee X' entirely, conducting daily work considerate of the greater good is possible and a worthy effort. Keeping a group on track for the sake of schedule, budget, and general expectations is appropriate in a professional work setting.

CHAPTER 5 | BEST PRACTICES

1. Listen more than you talk; when you do speak, it will be seen as important, valuable, or considerate rather than just to be heard.
2. Verify headsets are plugged in, turned on, and linked to the intended device.
3. When traveling, remember to pack power cords, a wireless mouse, and extra batteries; isolate potential sources of Wi-Fi as a backup plan.
4. Confirm power levels are adequate for the duration of expected use; have a charger nearby or offer updates at the start of the meeting (Chapter 6).
5. If working from a new, or less frequently utilized workstation, obtain Wi-Fi passwords and network connectivity in advance, not the minute before a call.
6. Install software updates on a Friday afternoon when call and email traffic is lower. The weekend is then available for troubleshooting.
7. Monitor actions of repeat offenders (time wasting chit-chatters, and/or IT deficient spotlight seekers). Where risk of repercussion is low, limit engagement.
8. If hosting, keep an eye on participant activity and engagement. As quality decreases, come to a close – sessions do not need to run the full length allotted.
9. Build a reputation of self-reliance - use automation tools for initial information before asking others.
10. When asked to join a call and low productivity is expected due to topic, timing, attendees, or the host, a 'tentative' accept provides an opt-out as a plan B; deploy where justifiable and not in excess.

CHAPTER 6 | MEETINGS AND CONFERENCE CALLS

"Success is where preparation and opportunity meet." – Bobby Unser

Jay Ferro, transformational leader and speaker, summarizes career development in three stages: wanting to be in the meeting, aspiring to run the meeting, and lastly, stopping at nothing to avoid the meeting altogether (Twitter, 2023). This abridged representation, while seemingly satirical, is pretty spot on in the experiences with senior members of staff I've worked with. Initially, the goal is to secure a seat at the table, to be seen and included. As confidence increases, you'll want to be heard, looked up to, admired. As responsibilities grow and schedules compress, weighing value for time spent takes center stage. Accommodating everyone and everything is unrealistic. Meetings are declined, or forwarded to proxies requesting their support to listen in and report back. Until rank or role is achieved where you may opt out with little risk, techniques included in this chapter touch on a range of situations. Recommended methods stress tested and deemed effective, are described in the following sections to utilize when needed.

Mid-career, acting on the advice of my now business partner, I shifted gears from commercial interior design to project management. The first meeting in the new industry was unlike no other I'd had up until that moment. Upon arrival, it was noticeably obvious that everyone seemed eager to speak. The host began promptly with a quick welcome and recap of the prior session. Expanding on expectations, the 'as per usual' standard described how each person would briefly share their update, round-robin style. After the last person spoke, the meeting organizer summarized agreed upon action items. A closing message conveyed that the subsequent touchpoint would be canceled as everyone was prepared and project efforts were well ahead of projections. No one looked surprised, but I was. The rapid-fire dialogue among colleagues could have been easily described as a well-scripted cast of a courtroom mini-series. Expressions on the faces of the attendees signaled satisfaction with the reward of an eliminated session.

Prior to the experience mentioned above, a Monday production meeting was the norm while trying my hand in the manufacturing sector. Too painful to forget, a group of zombie-like department leads filtered into the smallest conference room city code permitted, like clockwork each week. The lighting was harsh, the table cold, no windows to offer a glimpse of the outside world - any and all signs of life were void. As half inch thick reports, bound and highlighted, were handed out, a person muttered, 'I need another coffee'. A room of moderately paid individuals, who shared nothing in common except a work address, watched the clock or stared into space. Facilitation almost non-existent, the group muddled through their updates the moment someone else took a breath. Frequently, one individual would rise from the seat of a deteriorating faux-leather cushion. With a broken spirit, stifling the ability to stand at full height, the sound of the shuffle towards the door at least detracted from the notorious pen-clicker. No one bothered to look up in investigation; the cause of the interruption was the owner. Even ownership could not muster enough interest in the meeting, but rather than eliminate the time wasted, the requirement remained in place.

Calls and meetings have a similar storyline in that a time is set, a location indicated, and a range of content shared. Projected value is largely disproportionate to actual results for routine sessions maintained for historical sake alone. Expressed by Lencioni (2012, p.174), weekly staff meetings, a sort of 'corporate penance', exist as to check a box, satisfying division protocol. One study determined that the monthly average of 62 meetings translated to 31 hours (Puutio, 2023). Ironically, reoccurring gatherings are believed to signal collaboration and benefit, yet due to the increasing volume, there is little time to prepare in between, producing low to no value. Fewer meetings, ushering in quality over quantity can reimagine the daily routine, welcoming a moment for creativity and reflection between the call hop. Therefore, a proficiency in leading a group through a diverse agenda is an invaluable skill to focus on.

Meetings vetted as necessary stand a better chance of emerging with value when strategically timed. Coordinating a call on the first day back from an extended PTO might look good on paper, but I assure you, from witnessing call leaders digitally crash and burn, this is not recommended. Overwhelmed with emails, and out of touch with current status updates, it is better to refamiliarize prior to reconnecting with colleagues. Limiting calls and meetings on Mondays and Fridays is highly advisable. People are out of the office, or if present, either uninterested or unprepared - both situations tending to funnel conversations down the drain. Those subjected to small talk and superficial chatter are apt to decline the next invitation; return on investment, or ROI, for their needs unjustifiable based on the experience they had.

Unless deliberately stalling, keep sidebar commentary to a minimum allowing the main topics to retain center stage.

An agenda can make or break the session. Some may decline an invitation if the purpose is unknown or unclear. Meeting requests lacking mention of intent can be perceived as lazy, or an indicator of inexperience. At a minimum, include a few sentences, or three to four bullet points above the autogenerated dial-in specifics. Alongside reason and goal (Indeed, N.d.), list desired expectations for improved flow. This preview aids preparation of the audience mitigating being caught off guard, and saving face in the process. For optimal outcomes, attach relevant files or imagery related to the topic. According to Puutio (2023), leading with questions becomes a catalyst to worthwhile engagement. Sharing added detail lends credibility for bringing the group together. If discussion objectives involve a needed resolution, be prepared to mediate. While agendas are instrumental for efficiency, they mustn't be law, but a guide. The mark of an adept facilitator is the ability to pivot adjusting focus should changing conditions warrant. If time is better utilized in response to new information, by all means, assess the best path forward, and proceed.

It is unrealistic to believe you will be able to attend every call asked of you. Scheduling conflicts, illness, travel, and the like all routine factors to contend with. Fortunately, proactive options exist that are appropriate in a corporate setting, and appreciated by colleagues as well as clients. Where meetings compete for the same timeframe, Tulgan (2020) insists that a choice should be made, and the more important of the multiple meetings should be chosen. If an action item is required for the call(s) remaining, send your contribution to the organizer in advance. Alternatively, coordinate a representative to join in your place. In scenarios of not feeling well in the morning, chances are you will not feel better after working four hours in an upright position. It is prudent to hedge your bets and eliminate the risk all together. Canceling 30-minutes before a session is frustrating as some may have elected to take another call in lieu of the planned session. Declining minutes before the call equates to lost value on multiple counts instead of just one.

If conflicts are not an issue, but preparation is lacking, it is better to be forthcoming and request an optional time slot before a call or meeting begins. As for when to request another opportunity to connect, a few hours in advance should be at a minimum, however the following day is preferable. Conversely, if during a call you find that others are not prepared, recommend that the call be rescheduled, or if the group is large enough to continue a valuable discussion, excuse the person to drop from the line and use the time to do the actual work - either being a tricky situation where some mental gymnastics is required. In certain situations where deliverables are in jeopardy due to failures in accountability, boldness may be warranted. Before asking to reschedule, consider the repercussions of doing so. Are you routinely unprepared? Are you frequently unorganized, or experience issues accessing shared material needed to complete tasks? (Chapter 5) A one off, or highly infrequent, request for added time is largely deemed acceptable. I'd rather receive a colleagues' confession in advance, thereby avoiding taking time on a call to learn about their situation. If roles were reversed and _you_ extended an olive branch to an individual to spend the time on the task instead, it may be perceived as favoritism, or poor leadership. Each action has an effect – evaluate pros and cons before requesting or adjusting a planned session, or alternating requirements for some individuals.

When group engagement is requested, be thoughtful of who will be included and why. Assess the purpose of those invited and to what extent individual participation entails. These factors ensure the time taken to sit together is of merit. High-value guests such as C-suite and upper management, or subject matter experts (think engineers or lead techs) may decline to join if a full 1-hour is expected. Shifting the narrative to a focused, 15-minute touchpoint, enables a greater majority to join. For those who fall into such a group, offer that they participate at the first part of the call, or the last – as to support standing obligations. If faced with only two options – a lead engineer joins for 15-minutes or not at all, I will happily take what I can get. On the topic of who, be selective with the guest list. The larger the group, the increased likelihood for unknown unknowns, otherwise described as unforeseen matters that could not have been anticipated. Understand that the potential of a curve ball is eminent when groups are broad and include representation from multiple departments (cross-functional). Try to stay calm and speak to what you know. If completely lost for words or an answer, offer a timeframe giving assurance feedback will follow.

Consideration of others is critical. Dismissal of the time and energy of peers, leadership, or clients can adversely impact a personal brand (Chapter 1). Remaining on topic promotes focused discussion often resulting in succinct agreement. The sooner a decision is reached, the quicker a meeting can come to a close. One call, one topic. The 'hey while I have you on the line' mention is not a crowd pleaser. Although this tactic may eliminate an extra call, if attendees are only prepared for the main topic of conversation, pressing for more answers can lead to aggravation. I've found that allowing adequate time to respond often leads to better quality. Unless there are patterns of gross negligence of work, or lack of response, be patient. Should such a situation occur, attempt to resolve tastefully and outside of a public arena, as to avoid any misunderstanding of intentional criticism – obvious attempts at critique and correction while in a group setting will not be forgotten by the person on the receiving end. Phrase questions to encourage conversation and collaboration, not in an attempt to put someone on the spot.

Providing details to allow participants to prepare in advance is equally important as it is for those hosting the session. Mangia (2020) proposes that context over content is a best practice in meeting development etiquette. An overview of material that will be shared, and how colleagues can contribute effectively therein, should be included in the invitation. The overview, or context, sets expectations for the time together. Information can be relayed through file shares, images, or attachments. Attendees often respond best to background information, an executive summary if you will, simply due to competing responsibilities and mental bandwidth thereof. With this prework shared in a proactive manner, meetings and calls can be used for discussion and debate opposed to familiarization of backstory. As a point of caution, it is not reasonable to expect that the group will be proactive, some yes, but not all. The best you can do is supply essential context and clarify related expectations.

To attain clarity, quality content is necessary. An exact match to the human element does not exist as it relates to physical or cognitive labor, but remains vital for successful collaboration. For example, automated features that produce notes from audio are prone to flaws. Summaries more often than not may inadvertently omit necessary details to understand action items (Williams, 2024). In such situations, reliance on verbatim transcripts can lead to missed deadlines – auto generated notes lacking specifics on who is to do what, or by when, can also confuse communications between cross-functional teams. Generative AI, or machine-learning modeling, is the process of data prediction. Systems anticipate what is expected based on scores of examples already present online. The concept of a predictive "next-word" occurrence dating back to 1906 and referred to as the Markov chain – the namesake in relation to statistical techniques (Zewe,

2023). The machine is more or less self-trained as digital input grows exponentially from which to draw from. From faulty meeting minutes, however, accountability will likely suffer. Well documented call records tend to keep honest employees honest – meaning, on task due to visibility among peers. Even with increasing improvement in AI tools, outcomes are still fraught with imperfections – validate and fact check output routinely.

Comprehensive preparation requires discipline, but is achievable and commended. When you speak with confidence, others will respond through engaging dialogue. Familiarity of subject, paired with a structured outline, offers the best defense in mitigating wasted time and keeping the focus on objectives. If you are good on a call, it will be recognized. If seen as great on a call, it may be rewarded through increased inclusion. If delivery is deemed as outstanding, the exposure may serve as the catalyst, positivity impacting a career trajectory. The ability to communicate effectively can come down to self-assurance and style. Being articulate and having a tone that is pleasing to the ear - company stardom! In summary, as an attendee, strive for being a "meeting citizen" Tulgan (2020) or role model demonstrating respect for the group through active participation. Where hosting, monitor engagement levels and avoid going over scheduled - give back time when at all possible. A continuous drive to improve settings designed for collaboration is a worthwhile endeavor of the host and those in attendance.

CHAPTER 6 | BEST PRACTICES

1. Keep etiquette top of mind - be timely (professional) and engaged (considerate).
2. Avoid scheduling engagement the first day following PTO; you'll likely be overwhelmed with emails and out of touch with current status updates.
3. Limit invitations on Mondays and Fridays where possible; people are either out of the office, uninterested, or fatigued – conversations often end in small talk.
4. Superficial conversation can be seen as wasting time. Unless deliberately stalling, minimize sidebar conversations to focus on planned topics (Chapter 5)
5. Include agendas in invitations to set expectations and clarify intent.
6. Where attendance will not be possible due to a conflict, complete the task in advance or coordinate a representative in your place.
7. If unprepared, offer another time slot before the call begins. If observed that others on the call are not prepared, recommend that the call is rescheduled.
8. Phrase questions to encourage conversation, not in an attempt to put someone on the spot.
9. Remain on topic - the quicker items are discussed; the sooner meetings can end.
10. Treat digitally-generated content as a second set of data for cross-reference purposes to compare against what heard, or understood as important.

CHAPTER 7 | PRESENTATIONS

"There are always three speeches, for every one you actually gave. The one you practiced, the one you gave, and the one you wish you gave" - Dale Carnegie

As is the case with call and meeting facilitation, conveying information effectively in the form of a presentation, is an invaluable skill. Seeking a new role, requesting funding, advocating for a cause you feel strongly about, being able to articulate purpose and outcomes can generate a range of benefits. As such, I am routinely engaged with presenting on how to give a presentation. A more challenging scenario is when the group is diverse in tenure and responsibility level. An overview of the basics is well, too basic for seasoned professionals. Elaborative techniques on aligning content with posture is too overwhelming in concept for those who struggle with stage fright; keeping their head upright is a feat in and of itself. Written communication has the benefit of time to edit and construct messaging as intended. Verbal delivery requires the ability to speak with confidence from a place of topic expertise, all the while holding a group's attention. Arriving at an optimal balance of information, tailored to the intended audience, is a lifelong endeavor.

While the theory cannot be quantified, I believe I worked at a Fortune 500 company that inspired the 'mute-all' feature now a default in meeting software. On a late Monday afternoon, a group of 100 plus dialed into an online presentation for a service offering to compliment a recent product launch. An agenda saturated with information detailed methods selected to track and measure results of the business model. Twenty-minutes into the session, extremely loud snoring reverberated through the line. 'Hello, hello', in mayday-like fashion, the host pressed on, alas, there was no use. Whomever the guilty party was, they were illusive. The solution, with a sigh, was asking the group to hang up, and call back in. The returning attendees, less than half, was deemed too few to continue. This hibernation-bandit, still at large today, cost the organization thousands of dollars in lost productivity. A handful of missteps demonstrated in this example, all but guaranteed an unsuccessful session. Had the audience remained awake, an hour-long agenda on a Monday following lunch, would have challenged interest retention at some point in any case.

Conveying information, in an articulate and interesting manner, is a craft that can be continuously improved once comfortable. Glossophobia, or the fear of public speaking (Merriam-Webster) is derived from the Greek word for tongue - Glosso. The distress most feel when asked to speak in public is so great that many seek avoidance; the irony is that with exposure, unease is reduced. Statistically, 75 percent experience speech anxiety (Galle, 2017) claiming the top position of shared public phobias. To combat this aversion, a common saying comes to mind, 'practice, practice, practice'.

Volunteering to participate in classroom and workshop settings are excellent opportunities for refinement due to the low-risk environment provided. Both are ideal arenas for improving the art of speaking while perfecting stylist elements of a personal brand (Chapter 1). While in a classroom, should you miss an aspect of criteria in the prompt, a minor deduction in grade could be the outcome. In the 'real world', a poorly constructed proposal could result in losing a client or, if severe enough, a job. Any opportunity to practice across a network of advocates, think teachers, classmates, family, friends, should be utilized to improve basic delivery skills or hone techniques still in an experimental phase of your individual development.

An opening monologue of "I'm sorry" will not elicit sympathy from an audience if the speaker is unprepared, nervous, or incorrect. Quite the opposite, disclosure of anxiety devalues credibility as a speaker. What if this chapter began with, 'I have to apologize in advance that my presentation skills are not great, but here is what I know to help you improve yours' – most likely reading would come to a halt or expertise could be questioned. The same should be considered when joining a meeting or any conversation for that matter. Worth a moment to highlight a distinct difference, apologizing should not be confused with humility. Acknowledging the reality that you do not know everything is an indication of a healthy self-awareness, further described as emotionally intelligent (Goleman, 2020). Demonstration of such intellect should remain in use with day-to-day etiquette, whereas apologizing because you are not a master at something is unnecessary. Being brave and willing to share knowledge should be considered a gift extended to others. From this mindset, presenting from a state of "confidence, flexibility and resilience" (Riegel, 2019) supports gradual improvement.

Once realizing that presentations are inevitable when accepting a role in a corporate setting, comprehension of how to appeal to others is of significant importance. Striving for a connection is necessary as persuasion is not achievable solely with logic (Gallo, 2014). The audience must believe the message, relate to the material, or feel it is relevant to their role. Those who seem at ease in front of a group have invested a good deal of time in their personal development of public speaking. Speakers who leave a room silent for a few moments upon finishing a closing statement, equates to a very powerful moment a presenter should take great pride in. If you have attended a speaking engagement where the pace was comfortable and topic informative, take notes and learn when and where they are scheduled to speak again.

Regardless of level of preparation, or number of stunning visual, audiovisual glitches can quickly overshadow an otherwise quality presentation. Remote controls may be missing batteries, food may have upset a stomach, or a prototype could arrive damaged. Content and delivery remain controlled elements. When having comfort knowing you are prepared, outside factors and random disruptions can be addressed as they surface. A knack to roll with the punches is an indication of mastery; adeptness generated from the realization that continuous improvement is shaped from exposure. When such speakers are identified, listen and take notes or pivot points between themes, the pace of speech, and physical posture, or body language.

To paraphrase a famous quote by Plato, the wise speak when there is something worth saying, in contrast to a fool who speaks only to be heard. The importance of the old adage of 'think before you speak' never rang truer than when in a room, or on a call, with a large group. To that end, I'd be remiss to disregard the role of the audience. In a corporate setting, switching between both functions (presenter - audience) is commonplace and can occur within the same presentation, intentionally or not. When in the position of a participant, consider that active listening and involvement is hoped for by the speaker. Out of respect, the presenter must acknowledge that true engagement is draining and provide environments favorable to desired participation. The duration to strive for is 18-minutes; anything longer is scientifically proven to cause anxiety and "cognitive backlog" (Gallo, 2014, p.182). The audience, presumably receiving new information, must receive, digest, and later recall data shared. Surpassing the recommended timeframe incurs risk of disregard. In kind, those on the receiving side of a presentation should recognize the exertion of the presenter and do their best to remain on topic.

Prior to the fully remote work environment, sitting in cramped rooms, under fluorescent lighting, was the norm. In addition to a drab setting, imagery is generally dull.

Saturated with run-on sentences, in font selections too small to decipher. Disconnected from reality, voices that drone on, slide after stale slide of material already proven to have missed the mark, not an unfamiliar experience. Unfortunately, the digital working world echoes such patterns. To be fair, the ambitious-minded may go to great lengths to include variety, but often documents fall victim to repeated use, therefore seeming lackluster when repurposed and recycled. A determination to remain relevant with a measure of innovative perspective is the best we, the collective workforce, can attempt to achieve. Familiarity of subject matter, while being mindful of unnecessary disclosures (Chapter 5), enables intended outcomes.

AI can help solve a problem; it should not be considered as the solution in full. A goal of AI is to have machines learn from input of previous contributions. In time, input is stored, repurposed, and increases in quality. How to drive interest and maintain audience engagement occurs in real time, therefore reliant on human proficiencies. AI solutions can analyze and consolidate data, yet the success stemming from impromptu discussions while presenting to peers, clients, or other such stakeholders depends on the speaker's ability to pivot with immediacy. As such, regardless of how far technology has come, the art of giving an effective presentation remains an important skill to continue developing. Utilize AI solutions to refine material and enhance graphics, to achieve the desired tone and feel. Upon countless other tips found online, Van Edwards (2024) advocates for generative AI to be thought of as a communication copilot. Some features include opportunities to assess your presentation in return, offering suggested modifications to evaluate for inclusion in the end result. Much like presenting in a classroom for a grade, AI can act like a digital professor offering advice on pace (timing), level of anticipated audience comprehension, and perception the message may relay. Adjusting word choice can fine tune the final delivery, resonating as preferred or needed.

I have performed countless presentations, and participated in even more. Results as wide-ranging as the subjects themselves, the quote included in this chapter substantiated. Contemplation of the 'what if' or 'if only' all too poignant as we are always our biggest critics. Reflection after the fact however serves as an educational component to enhance speaking proficiency. An exercise that does not need to be exhaustive or time consuming, but treated as instrumental in personal growth. A quick assessment of what could have gone better isolates areas or techniques to avoid in the next opportunity; conversely, identifying what went well aids further development. If there were more questions than anticipated, graphics may be too sparse, or key points over simplified, reducing comprehension.

While there are multiple differences between sectors, markets, and company type, one constant can be counted on without fail – numerous presentations. As the volume of which in corporate settings is never ending, there will not be a shortage of opportunities to improve techniques. While developing public speaking skills, experiment often and fine-tune as needed. Be open for constructive feedback and request advice from those considered as extraordinary facilitators. I applaud each and every moment an individual spends in research, but practical experience, on the spot, in front of the mic, is the best teacher.

CHAPTER 7 | BEST PRACTICES

As the Presenter
1. If held in-person, review the room – is there sufficient furniture, lighting, and equipment (chairs, tables, notepads, pens)
2. Before the group arrives, test hardware and software – audio, visual, lighting, batteries in remotes, charge/power sources (Chapter 5 and 6).
3. Secure a backup copy (USB drive, digital cloud); computers can be damaged, lost, run low on power, or be compromised by a virus.
4. Set expectations at the start – provide an overview of subject matter, intent, and duration; when longer than 30-minutes, inform the group that a break will occur.
5. Inform the group if Q&A is suitable during, or if should be held until the end.
6. Pause between slides where imagery is powerful or content is dense.
7. Maintain awareness; if obvious that the group is unfocused, wrap up early or offer a micro break.
8. Common sense is unfortunately not that common. Keep bulky jewelry to a minimum. It is disruptive and avoidable. Save the hardware for a concert.
9. Utilize AI tools with caution – treat as a source of enhancing material – presentations are best received when felt to be authentic and compelling.
10. Effort spent on preparation should align with the importance level of the meeting. Make the time to practice and evaluate.

As an Attendee
1. Evaluate what you need and expect from the session in advance.
2. Offer support to the facilitator, bring in chairs, take notes, monitor the clock, etc.
3. Jot down questions during the presentation, but wait until Q&A is offered to ask. Most likely questions will be answered throughout material shared.
4. Do not interrupt the speaker unless it is truly warranted - time is running long, someone is needed urgently, audio/visual issues not observed by the host, etc.
5. Be prepared to participate; remain on topic when offering feedback or a question.
6. Consider tone and timing of comments - position questions as clarifying
7. If arriving late, quietly blend into the conversation and engage when appropriate – do not interrupt only to offer a monologue as to why you were late (Chapter 5)
8. Not only silence cell phones, but put them away in a pocket or bag. Be attentive.
9. Multi-tasking is often mistaken to be an effective use of time; however, quality suffers. If something else is that important, prioritize and decline to join.
10. Reflect on the experience in comparison to the notes taken beforehand. Were needs and expectations met? If not, is your experience worth sharing with the host or was your attendance not actually necessary?

CHAPTER 8 | TAKE ACTION

"The secret of getting ahead is getting started" – Mark Twain

Navigating through tasks, even if details are limited, is necessary for the sake of productivity. Yet taking the first step is typically the most difficult, as variables can be numerous and results broadly unknown. Mere predictions of what lies ahead steers many into a state of procrastination or worse yet, becoming "frozen in indecision" (Yiu, 2019). Common tactics to stall advancement are coordinating excessive calls or extending deadlines without justification. Not knowing where to start when confronted with a blank page or unfamiliar setting, can be intimidating for some, yet exhilarating for others. Regardless of classification between the two, moving forward in good faith is to be commended over inaction due to apprehension. As commonly utilized in academic endeavors, creating an outline is a good first step. Organize details based on what is known, with the intention of building from the original framework as additional information is acquired or received. Corporate output is largely based on collaborative and iterative engagement. Course correction allows incremental movement towards achievement of desired results.

My first experience in a Fortune 100 arose from luck and timing. Following a relocation abroad, I applied for any and all openings remotely close to the skills and education attained. One in particular caught my eye as a 'native English speaker' was listed as the primary requirement. The organization's urgency to fill the position in my favor. Accepting the offer, it was later learned that the purpose of the role was budget retention. Keeping a seat filled, ensuring headcount retention, shaped an early lesson in corporate environments (Chapter 9) – money was spent as not to lose it in the following budget year. The role was interesting, but the caliber, a league well above my comfort level. About a month in, I was asked if translation of marketing material from English to French was possible. Without hesitation, I replied "oui" – part of my dazzling vocabulary (which consisted of a few words resulting from dinner table conversations when my sister took High School French). The department lead smiled and said, very clever! Apparently, I 'knew' more French than he, but alas, not enough to complete the task.

Taking action was paramount. Extension of my contract was fueled by a desire of continued professional growth, and in the following example, caffeine. Off to the café, media requiring translation in hand, a round of cappuccinos were purchased. Ceremoniously and head high, I spotted the French speaking table, distributed the beverages, and waited. As the sips ensued, eyebrows raised, however the currency power of caffeine resulted in victory. Voilà! Two variations of content surfaced, along with an open invitation to host coffee service anytime translation services were required. As new assignments surfaced, I answered the call. Should a leader state, 'we need that in Italian', the reply, an all-purpose Italian word Prego! would do the trick. Career-enabling moments, borne from relationship management techniques, and good ole' fashioned hospitality, a winning formula. As the initial 3-month contract extended into a 4-year opportunity, a sort of inner-office United Nations formed. This new alliance was never taken for granted.

In contrast, in a prior role as a design assistant for a model home venture, I attempted to tackle requests without guidance as comradery was revealed as superficial. The associate degree on my shelf at home did not prepare me for the cultural environment of a multi-generational team, within the highly competitive field of commercial interior design. With limited positions in lead creative roles, it was obvious I was on my own. Hours were lost searching for material, products, and resources others could pull out of thin air. Discouraged at the onset, then determined to prove my worth, I had to re-educate myself the only way I knew how - research. Seeking out local trade shows and conferences to attend, slowly but surely, a once limited network grew into an impressive range of contacts. Combined with pouring over magazine articles and speaking with designer showroom attendees, my design acumen developed.

Quality improved and colleagues took notice. I firmly believed then and still do today, that the tactics of blatant ignorance of junior associates was to hinder motivation. Disappointing for those of a creative mindset. Being on the receiving side of this unhealthy mentality, I took an oath then and there that I would never treat a team as a competitor. As individuals, each person is unique and can stand on their own strengths and career trajectory. Rhoten (2023) describes the phenomenon of a scarcity mindset for those who are hesitant to extend support or recognition in fear that limited success is achievable for themselves. There is a bond unlike anything else when you find a person of similar mindset who echoes this work ethic. Agreeing that collaboration allows success for both sides, I can say with all sincerity, that upholding my oath holds firm today. Identify your own swim lane, and cheer others along as they progress in theirs.

Pivotal growth through mentorship outside of the office was deemed as a great solution for integration into the design world. Capitalizing on what you know, then slowly blending in new information will increase traction – moving the needle, even if ever so slightly. Industry professionals are vast and when timing is appropriate, interviews or speed mentor sessions are excellent opportunities to cover a range of topics. These brief, yet focused conversations enable "high potential development" (Haeger, n.d.) for all participants. When necessary to call upon your own ambition, seek tools and resources online related to the task. Very little is new and more often than not, your situation has been encountered, at least to some magnitude. Any deliverable, large or small, whether a presentation deck to an exhaustive report, an outline or template in existence can give you a running start, inspiring a custom framework to accommodate unique parameters.

Performing under pressure will occur throughout a career. For complex tasks, conduct a risk mapping to expose as many factors as possible at the onset. Standards such as SWOT, Risk Register, Risk Profile are widely utilized in the corporate setting. As methods such as these are commonplace, online examples are vast. Experimenting with the various options will eventually lead to a preferred approach. While moving too quickly can add risk, avoidance of the inevitable out of fear, can be as, if not more, detrimental. Not only could projects and initiatives suffer from lack of advancement, but career turmoil can ensue as well. Cast as being indecisive or not proactive may cause senior leaders to question ability and fit within the capacity assigned (Sutton and Rao, 2014). Finding a balance of action and risk is better facilitated once the concept of course correction is understood and implemented as a daily protocol.

Stakeholder engagement is crucial to achieve larger goals (Chapter 4). Pooling resources and playing from strengths isolated within a group generates creativity – a catalyst of progression. Understanding how to complete tasks in an order necessary to accommodate a critical path, or favorable sequence for best results, can help guide a conversation. The process of course correction is highly important to understand and utilize and application can occur at various stages, although it is often a midstream tactic. Forming a starting point is a separate matter altogether. Operating outside of comfort zones broadens proficiencies and challenges confidence. This feeling of 'being uncomfortable' is not desired, but at times necessary as a playbook for each and every scenario is nonexistent. One part self-reliant, one part embracing a sense of adventure could arrive at a positive mindset of picturing the "best possible outcome" (Parker, 2023). It is astonishing to witness the quick nature colleagues and clients come to rely upon those who just make it happen.

AI can support a range of everyday tasks and is continually evolving. To what extent AI will transform roles and job functions is yet to be seen, but increased integration is a widely accepted notion. Factors such as ease of use and lower costs remain key drivers in the growing demands placed on technology (Suleyman, 2023). However, upskilling an existing workforce is noted as an uphill climb for corporations (Hall, 2023). As a result, those who take an early adopter stance may find unexpected opportunities. Learning more about company-approved AI platforms showcases an ability to acclimate to change, thus setting an example for added acceptance amongst peers. While individual expertise comes with time, starting somewhere is necessary. Therefore, incremental exposure from tool experimentation leads to enhanced proficiencies. From automating reporting to digitally recorded meeting notes, AI should no longer be thought of as reserved for the IT department, or engineer minded. Consider the positive impact on personal branding (Chapter 1) when innovation can be effectively demonstrated, highlighting the added value you bring to the organization.

Effective advancement is predicated on accountability and expertise, paired with self-assurance. Many corporate folks enjoy planning phases given the stakes are at the lowest point of an assignment or initiative. Time remains on the clock, budgets are not exhausted, nor are resources. Energy and optimism are usually high and discussions are generally solution-based, brainstorming exercises. The shift to execution, the hard work of actually checking boxes, is a visible activity – if nothing happens for an extended period, clients or managers WILL notice. You can only talk so long before someone in charge speaks up in a meeting, questioning when results will be seen. Individuals intimidated by implementation search for ways to avoid obligations. As production is necessary at some point in a project or initiative, be cautious of those who elect to delegate throughout a conversation, or decline to join due to obligations elsewhere. The ability to distinguish reasonable needs in assistance opposed to intentionally stalling is amplified as trends continue to form. There is a stark difference, the main variation is a signal of distress versus a defensive front shaped under pretense.

Handling each personality type varies and pending your capacity (lead, supportive, sponsor, etc.), lend guidance appropriate to influence or authority level. Herman (2018) discusses confronting situations through the application of a sequential method of assessment, analyzation, articulation, followed by adapting. This approach can be treated as a tool in the evaluation process arriving at an informed choice with what you know while considering what could be missing in the equation. The missing link could be one of a hundred elements, but low to no value will materialize without exerting energy in some capacity. Heath *et al.*, (2022, p.104) describe the "cumulative outcome of common actions" as it pertains to the familiarity of assessing what has transpired to guide the next step. Recontextualized into productivity, what primary action triggers the next and so on. Whether attempting to reach Point B from Point A, incremental steps are necessary regardless if the duration is known or an approximation. Until tested and proven, the results are figurative and thereby of little worth.

When it comes to choices, consideration of associated consequences is absolutely necessary and recommended. Doing nothing to circumvent making the wrong choice is already the wrong choice. When stakes are high, pausing for additional data or figures prior to proceeding is warranted, however, an expiration date on the path forward, or a Go/No Go decision, should be instated. It is illogical to wait until all pertinent details are known. Lean on the process of course correction ever mindful that corrective measures are limitless – reflect, recalibrate, and repeat. The fundamental ingredient to achieving objectives is a willingness to drive action. Echoing the sentiment of Mark Twain, a few parting words by Richard Branson (2011, p.197) "You can only get into first place by giving something a try".

CHAPTER 8 | BEST PRACTICES

1. Have confidence in your skillset; it is unique and impossible to replicate.
2. Work from the mindset of being a solution provider and problem solver.
3. Do not immediately strike down a task outside of your qualifications; assess resources to determine if success is achievable in the required timeline.
4. Build relationships before they are needed and be genuine when requesting support or guidance at a later date.
5. For complex tasks, conduct a risk mapping to expose variables based on what is known at the time. (SWOT, Risk Register, Risk Profile, etc.)
6. Large initiatives require collaboration – either with internal or external colleagues. Get comfortable working in a team or group setting.
7. When overwhelmed, take a step back or switch activities - answers may show themselves when looking elsewhere opposed to focusing on a time constraint.
8. Consider the advice of Herman (2018), assess, analyze, articulate, and adapt. when confronted with new challenges.
9. Isolate ways to introduce AI functionality into routine tasks; automation saves time which in turn, saves money.
10. Deciphering between those in need of support from others who intentionally hold back progress is essential (Chapter 5)

CHAPTER 9 | CORPORATE ENVIRONMENTS

"Having a clear goal makes it easier to navigate the unexpected" - Sean Peek

Setting clear goals is a fundamental theme embedded within the publications written by Stephen Covey. If not familiar with the *7 Habits of Highly Effective People*, it is highly likely that at some point in your corporate career, this quintessential narrative will surface. Navigating environments as an enduring quest to strike a balance in productivity is essential to achieve individual aspirations. The rub being that a handful of associates encountered along the way will not possess this mindset, all the while firmly asserting, they do. How to decode spiteful character traits, and diffuse potentially harmful conversations with colleagues who work tirelessly to cast a poor light on others, is a corporate environment reality. Once accepted, adapting to a range of circumstances can lead to a fulfilling tenure. At select points along the way, timing may just be in your favor when least expected.

With a hot off the press diploma in hand, I set out to build a new career. Accepting an offer to support a prestigious conglomerate, I naively believed immaturity of colleagues was in the past. I was wrong. In fact, the bigger the corporation, the more intense the competition. In hindsight, this should have been obvious, yet, an exchange transformed any remaining morsel of hope into a sobering affirmation of corporate reality. Determined to pursue a Master's degree only a month following my undergrad, I enrolled in a local program close to the office for ease of commuting. After attending night courses for the previous five years, what would two more matter. It was realized, however, that I would need to depart in the late afternoon two days a week due to limitations in class scheduling. My supervisor had no issues with the arrangement, given the ability to manage time efficiently demonstrated on my part. I maintained the routine for a month, then opted for a more robust program that was also fully remote.

On what would have been one of the days I would have typically departed early, our regional manager paid a visit to the team. The only open seat in the office was adjacent to my desk; certainly, it was expected a conference room would be used. They walked by, viewed the open desk beside mine and extended a warm greeting - "Hello Nicole, anyone sitting here?" I was elated, but not surprised as I've found very little occurs by chance in the corporate world. Perhaps curious of the new employee as to keep apprised of the pulse of the workforce. Roughly

30-minutes after the time I would have normally left for class, a colleague that was displeased with the broad strokes of recognition received for my contributions marched right over to my desk. Looking down at their watch, it was questioned why I was still in the office as I was 'always' leaving mid-day to take care of other obligations. My suspicions confirmed - the gloves were finally off. Ears perking up, the regional manager slowed their keystrokes. The air grew thick. Had I just been challenged to an office duel?

Composed and actually quite pleased once realizing the opportunity of the moment, I met the gaze of my challenger. Proudly, I proclaimed with assurance, "Oh, you haven't heard! I transferred to an international program, specializing in our industry, and the classes are fully remote. I can support my Master's degree in the evening and on weekends". A bit deflated, but not yet satisfied with the outcome, subsequent commentary ensued with questions about the intensity level of coursework and how I was so certain it was achievable with work obligations. My reply in turn contained mention of earning my undergrad with honors, working full time, all the while supporting multiple direct reports. These elements were proof enough in my view, but to cap off the exchange for good measure, I iterated how beneficial the added exposure within our business category would be.

As the colleague conceded, the pace of the regional manager's keystrokes resumed to previous levels and all was calm for the remainder of the afternoon. Demonstrating quick thinking, I affirmed my brand centered on professionalism through appropriate self-assertion. The careful positioning of replies in response to their attempt of a negative burn, fizzled and dissolved. My academic career was not questioned in front of leadership thereafter. The opportunity to advertise the initiative taken in personal development was ideal. Additionally, the division lead learned about my recent accomplishments, as well as my continued aspirations. In parallel, they observed, firsthand, my calm demeanor under pressure, handling an abrupt line of accusatory questioning, and frankly an unprofessional dig. The exchange was better than any script, or pitch I could have drafted to increase visibility. Two months later the regional leader invited me to join a digital conference as a guest speaker representing our client. The audience involved 50+ senior leaders. I spent two hours preparing for a 10-minute segment - well worth it.

Companies are dependent on human resources much to the same level as consumer consumption. As companies respond to accommodate market fluctuation, teams alter in response. Some avoid rowing in the same direction, or disregard professional etiquette in full, thereby rocking the proverbial boat. Just as allies must be chosen wisely, which battles are fought should receive the same level of evaluation. Sometimes it is not just business, it does get personal. If the company is where you'd like to be, respond to adversaries in a stoic manner and press on. Those in opposition will eventually lose steam in the attempt to keep up. When considering organizations, remember that interviews serve two functions – to determine applicant qualifications and for the potential candidate to decide if the business is of interest in return.

Large companies advertise buzz words around training and opportunity for growth to attract top talent. Tools are only of value if utilized, and if left unguided with how to implement such an array of resources, the vast majority of the employee base may discount them altogether. Bossidy and Charan (2002, p. 118) note that, for those in supervisory roles, 40 percent of time should be dedicated towards human resources, inclusive of initial selection and continual development. In reality, managers who are inundated with conference calls and reporting find difficulty allocating time required for mentorship. Career development is often classified as extracurricular, a nicety as time allows; this mindset can lead to dissatisfaction of the workforce. When superiors are engaged with corrective and motivational pursuits of the, let's refer to them as 'Chapter 5 offenders', the balance of the team is placed on the back burner. Left to their own devices, self-driven innovation may take shape, but the lack of equal time received by that of their peers will not be forgotten. If someone is truly struggling with genuine issues, then by all means, lend support. In my observations, however, unfortunate souls of constant duress are often the same few. Employees consistently front and center of another predicament, command attention, thus monopolizing senior leaders. Resentment often forms within those capable of productivity without self-induced drama.

Increasingly prevalent the larger a company is, some may accept an assignment only to take the credit for 'saving the day', knowingly unable to fulfill the need due to insufficient knowledge or a schedule conflict. Being on the receiving side of colleagues who have delegated work without sincere gratitude, it is now easier to recognize, thereby increasing the chance of evading a similar ordeal. Pending the exchange with a peer, apply one of the below approaches for a graceful out. In doing so, a political acumen and individual confidence is demonstrated; traits that workplace bullies detest. While the successful punt of a task may require a few attempts for improved polish in delivery, eventually success can ensue. No longer deemed low hanging fruit, opportunistic coworkers opt to try their luck elsewhere.

- **Bartering** - accept the task in exchange for another that is equal in scope, time and complexity, but that is less glamorous or less visible to leadership.
- **Let's collaborate** – reply with commentary that a series of calls for check-ins and to obtain feedback for the task will follow; a possible outcome may be an aggressive reply, exclaiming that the task does not require group effort. When able to provide a valid counter to this argument, the matter may seemingly dissolve or be retracted as seen as too much to 'deal with'.
- **Over engineer** – offer to assist with the request and highlight the pre-work necessary before you can begin, thus still a level of involvement by the requestor before the preferred hand off.

When tasks originate from a manager, or other member of staff with seniority, opting out, or bartering is not often realistic. Seeking clarification or support **is** however appropriate, potentially casting a spotlight on ulterior motives of those looking to dodge workload.

- **Highlight Commitments** - request an order of priority from existing tasks already assigned shedding light on existing obligations.
- **Be highly inquisitive** – respond with a precisely crafted line of questioning, framed as increasing your clarification (as more often than not, matters will not be clear). Chances are the asker does not fully understand needs themself, but will be reluctant to admit it. Magically, time will be made to complete the task once they decipher what exactly the task is or put to the side, deemed no longer relevant.
- **The 'Follow up'** – affirm the request in written detail, and expand the audience by way of the CC (copy) function. This is a bold move as you are literally communicating to others that you have been asked to help and expect to be recognized for your contributions.

A word of caution! The last option should be used sparingly as repercussions are likely to surface should you have the unfortunate situation of reporting to a passive-aggressive manager. An email that feels good in the moment, or an assertive comment in your defense, may be taken out of context or blown out of proportion, potentially classified as combative behavior. Before you type or speak, recall this particular section and let me, your Corporate Coach, be your conscience – tapping you on the shoulder. Have you thought this through? Can you move into another role? What options do you have? If no viable option is arrived at, it may be time to leave all together. Period. Lose the battle, but win the war. Some may thrive in arenas of business politics, using the setting as a means to conceal petty behaviors under the guise of inexperience or naivety. Such a person is usually highly aware of what the 'right thing' to do may be, but chooses the 'wrong thing' simply for sport as to watch others flop and fail. The energy expended would be better used by just performing the role.

Companies have favoritism. Understand that this reality is part of 'the game' - unfortunate, yet true. Belief that hard work and dedication alone will catapult a career may lead to disappointment and fatigue. Instead, focus energy on building a well-rounded network to understand who will work as hard as you do, opposed to others looking out for themselves. Taking note of phony colleagues and their intentions, which may not be verbalized, is equally important. It is not out of the ordinary that once skills are observed in action, envy and unhealthy competition ensue. Attempting to make you look poorly in front of upper management through comments or questions outside of your strengths is a common ploy of colleagues with a self-serving agenda. Individuals unconcerned with the "success of the greater good" (Sutton *et al.,* 2014, p.148) surface in time, becoming visible for the wrong reasons. Developing a proficiency in understanding the bigger picture of an organization helps determine when to blend in and where appropriate to stand out. While working through the red tape of bureaucracy ever present in such a workplace, a diplomatic approach may light the way to the high road.

Decidedly impressive, the range of AI abilities primarily involve task optimization, such as building and sorting data or generating content from a specific set of instructions. Industries inclusive of "cognitive labor" (Lee, 2018) are still reliant on expertise gained from years of exposure. Meaning, how to adapt in unscripted situations remains in human favor. The present state of AI is therefore regarded as restricted, or narrow (Lee, 2018). It is prudent, however, to acknowledge that increasing proficiencies, adapting to resources is a best practice to retain a level of relevancy. To sustain a competitive advantage, companies must also adopt a digital mindset. In doing so, it will be expected that employees follow suit

(Lakhani and Ignatius, 2023). Areas where AI can complement initiatives with low risk at reduced cost are sure to increase as platforms are tested for quality output. From this realization, AI utilization should be considered as a tool to "augment and increase productivity" (Pang, 2020). Alternatively, those who lag on AI adoption may find themselves disregarded as organizations continue to value-engineer roles.

In connection to advancement, the final reality to highlight is the bottom line. When budgetary cuts are required, resources are depersonalized for the sake of the company. You become a number. Regardless of your strengths, contributions, and track record, the cost of business can cost you your job. A brutal statement, I admit, however, this book would be incomplete in essential corporate survival insight if not mentioned. It is prudent to reserve a level of physical and mental capacity to deploy where necessary. If running on empty consistently, you will be unprepared to respond to a disruptive occurrence such as a reorg, merger, or the like. As it relates to success in the workplace, blue chip positions often make their way to individuals who maintain a company first, professional always work ethic. If you take nothing else from this chapter except one concept, understand this - little in business is coincidental.

CHAPTER 9 | BEST PRACTICES

1. Understand the business and industry of the company applying to, or working for.
2. Consider the repercussions of actions as well as the consequences of inaction. How you move forward alters the course of a project, relationship, etc.
3. Determine and live by your own individual standards and aspirations. It is acceptable to take cues from those you admire, but professional goals are unique and must be treated as such.
4. Observe and evaluate; there are multitudes of activities and individuals in an organization – be selective in engagement. Be open to ideas, yet cautious with choices as each action triggers the next.
5. Give your best, but not everything as to retain physical and mental capacity.
6. Training and education for continuous self-development should not be overlooked and is your responsibility.
7. Accept that companies have favoritism. Decide when to stand up, when to stand down, and when to walk out the door.
8. Just as companies look for ways to produce results in less time, you should do the same demonstrating a strategic mindset of innovative adoption.
9. Budget cuts are a reality; consider ways to prepare today to adapt tomorrow such as increasing your value (skills) and network (alliances in all departments).
10. Just like careers unfold, business objectives shift. Strategic choices in your professional path should account for corporate needs as well as your own.

CHAPTER 10 | PERFORMANCE REVIEWS

"Without reflection, we go blindly on our way." - Margaret J. Wheatley

Performance evaluations are an annual exercise that are a part of the corporate landscape - signaling a time for personal reflection. The past 12-months are summed up in a brief compilation, justifying decisions made and reflecting on effects thereof to guide future choices. Across various companies and industries, I have learned a great deal about capitalizing on personal strengths and what areas remain for self-improvement. In conjunction, from a range of leaders and those in positions of managerial oversight, it is now easier to identify allies from adversaries. To put it plainly, just because someone believes they are a fair and just leader, the proof will surface as respect is given, or resignations are tendered by subordinates. Annual reviews offer a moment of examination for an employee, as well as management in return. Constructive feedback received during related conversations, thus at the core of improved professional mapping.

My first performance review received while at a commercial interior design studio still resonates today.

The process stung at the time, but the experience was regarded as instrumental in career advocacy development. After supporting requests without hesitation, traveling monthly, and incurring weekly overtime, my review was that of a 0.15% raise (for context, 3% was the average at the time). The amount laughable, worth less than the paper the review was written on. In spite of the fact that all other team leads were complementary in regards to my efforts, I was told the amount aligned with what they (my manager) had experienced. Curious, yet convenient for the owner, all reviews issued on my team were low, meaning less financial outlay. Fully aware of the value provided to the firm, I set an appointment to speak with the vice president. The ultimatum proposed included reporting to a different team lead effective immediately, and after one month, I would be reevaluated. I expected that any increase in pay would be retroactive from the past month, and my former supervisor investigated for foul play. If my proposal was declined, a two-week notice would be given. Four weeks later, a 5% raise was received; holding steady to beliefs worked in my favor.

Another tale of very different circumstances is one of not deserving a promotion, but demanding nothing less. An annual review conducted with an inherited member of staff left quite an impression as vivid as if it just occurred. To paraphrase, but essentially, a statement made was to the effect of "I need to be promoted to a managerial role to demonstrate what a valuable employee I could be". I sat staring into the eyes of this direct report, baffled and saddened; the combination of which, to my benefit, seemed to have formed a sort of expressionless poker face. The eyes of the employee grew wider as I digested this seemingly abrupt and confusing declaration. I determined that the best approach in response to this passive-aggressive comment was one of equal directness. It was explained that their statement alone 'demonstrated' that they were not ready for a leadership position. Deliberately underperforming as a form of leverage to gain advancement is a poor showing of character.

Aligning a career trajectory to a unique set of strengths or preferences is as rewarding as it is taxing. Honest self-reflections are generally mirrored by your manager if touchpoints (1-1's) are maintained. The result is having a good idea of where you stand; performance reviews are thus not completely out of left field, but as I shared at the top of this chapter, such instances are also not out of the question. The illogical seem to find ways to form logical explanations in their mind. Certainly, this is an odd process that allows a single, subjective opinion to define a years' worth of contribution, but that is the reality of the corporate environment in most cases. Following a standardized formula, often a proprietary model integrated through company protocols, attempts to achieve accurate accounts of one's conduct and productivity level.

When career development is the topic of discussion, let accomplishments speak for themselves. Utilize the time with your manager to highlight how added value was brought to align with business objectives. From process enhancements reducing administrative time, to increased market share, details and context are expected and encouraged. Throughout the year, eliciting praise and lobbying for recognition may be seen in a negative light as attention seeking. However, when appropriate such as specifically speaking to your involvement, information validating claims is expected, and by some organizations, encouraged. Some companies utilize measures such as peer to peer reviews, self-rating scales, and reflection surveys. Resulting numbers provide quantifiable data and whether viewed as pro or con, such methods to distinguish one employee from the next within the workforce, is commonplace in corporations.

A larger benchmark in determining overarching success, is that of Key Performance Indicators or KPIs. (Note - this is an acronym that will become part of your corporate vocabulary in time if it is not already). These data points serve as a guide, or benchmark, in which to measure service levels of large groups of resources (teams) or initiatives (project/programs). Due to the impact of KPIs on overall success, these indicators are tied to performance of individuals as well as the collective. How large the impact will depend on a variety of factors, like size and duration of the item the KPI monitors. But if severely falling short of expectations, bonuses or merit increases might be eliminated in full. A blow to those who performed to the best of their ability, but were outnumbered by the underperformers and the uninterested. Understand KPIs and speak with management for guidance when new to a company or role as no two KPIs are alike and are weighted differently. Deciphering on your own accord is not advisable as incorrect interpretations may lead down a rabbit hole working towards something unnecessary or incorrect.

From a managerial perspective, genuinely caring for another's well-being is proven through action. Did the person feel heard, understood, looked after? Annual meetings offer a chance to review the year in a consolidated view, focusing on significant wins and "corrective" areas isolated for additional development (Laurinavicius and Main, 2023). This is also the appropriate time and place for open dialog concerning deficiencies that if left unresolved may compromise trust, engagement, or promotional opportunities. Regardless of relationship type, an open line of communication is pivotal. Each side must participate in a forthright manner. Through mutual respect, an employee-manager dynamic will either make or break the path forward. Whether on the giving or receiving end of the conversation, engage in an honest, yet considerate, manner and settle for nothing less in return.

Employees who met expectations may receive up to a 4.6 percent raise during annual reviews (Miller, 2022). This being almost a half point higher than years past, demonstrating the attempt for employers to remain competitive in their market segment. In larger organizations, however, awarding each employee a merit increase at the top range is not realistic. When an assessment of 'far exceeds' is received, the percentage can be higher. However, significant pay bumps are typically reserved for promotions or when changing jobs (Perman, 2023). While promotion-based merit increases spruce up a bank account balance, increases in responsibility and potentially travel may follow. Nothing is free – more money can equate to more time demanded. Going into an annual review on the heels of a stellar year, consider your reply should more be asked of you. Compensation matching role demands may be more than fair, but considering how quality of life could be impacted should be accounted for in advance. Not to be disregarded either is that when switching between organizations for the sake of a higher salary, seniority is a factor to take into account (Perman, 2023). Are you willing to be the rookie, again? The upside may be more seniority alongside higher earnings, thereby outweighing tenure to an extent. Again, evaluate the various strings that may be attached before making a jump.

Seeking innovative solutions, building a business case, presenting to your manager and securing a budget for implementation of an innovative idea, could lead to a promotion, or at minimum a favorable mention in an annual assessment. Fulfilling a function in a secondary capacity to prove need is an appropriate way to demonstrate drive, confidence, and leadership. A customized position to fill a void is achievable if a business justification is sound. If it is felt that proving a role first is necessary, or that a pay increase should take effect before the merit of such action is validated, expect to stay in your current area of responsibility. Those of a self-serving nature, who are willing to risk a red mark on their personal brand may elect to expedite career growth and devise a plan without putting in the time. I have seen such plans develop, surface, and fail; success is often immediate, but the smoke eventually clears and delivering on a bill of goods from the polished sales pitch is required. As skills and knowledge lack for the role assumed, haze from the illusion of grandeur turns into focus and seen for what it is – residual ash from the bridges burnt along the way.

When work contributions target the overall good of a team or organization, and a glowing review and potential promotion is anticipated, be prepared to accept or graciously decline on the spot. In situations where you decide to pass on an opportunity, understand that subsequent offers may not follow in the current division, or company at all for that matter. If family or health matters inhibit an ability to just say 'yes', be candid without oversharing every detail. This tactic may soften the blow of your choice to decline while demonstrating future interest. Honesty can turn the conversation from a dead-end deal breaker to a strategic planning session. Alternatively, if the capacity assigned is too easy, ascending to the next level of responsibility may be justified generating a reasonable topic to propose during a year-end assessment. Either way, roles are not forever and conditions are ever changing on your part as well as the organization itself. The key is to remain in a capacity long enough to make the determination if adjustments are possible and worth the effort, or if leaving the company altogether is best.

Where favoritism lacks, an attitude of entitlement or complacency will get you nowhere fast. Instead, treat career growth and corresponding evaluations with a mindset of giving more than asked, and working harder than those who work for you, in cases of managing direct reports. Limit productivity to exhaustion day in day out, but understand some weeks will be more demanding than others. Maintaining such a balance promotes a small bank of contingent energy to draw upon when a critical deadline surfaces. Before joining a manager in reviewing contributions made throughout the year, reflect on how you would answer the question of why should you be promoted? Because a response of 'increased pay and authority is necessary before performing well' in a role an individual is already being paid for is the wrong answer. Some may argue that such a frank statement stems from looking out for one's' best interest; a better approach is demonstration of worth through results elevated beyond expectations.

Thought to induce optimal performance, organizations go to great lengths to generate playbooks, or consolidated user guides related to company-specific processes and procedures. Some senior level executives believe such documents are sufficient enough to work autonomously with successful completion of an assigned task. In reality, playbooks are best considered as a reference to refresh your memory on processes not frequently performed. When learning 'from scratch', a more in-depth training protocol is needed and should be provided by your organization, manager, or team. In such situations, asking appropriate questions sparingly is acceptable. Expecting colleagues, managers, and clients to accommodate questions in detail is unrealistic. If not in a training or classroom, it will be expected that you have a general understanding – at least the very basics. AI integration into daily practice can serve as a lifeline for research and increased proficiencies related to your role and industry. If consistent weakness is observed, self-proclaimed qualifications may come into question at the time of annual reviews. If poor performance severely impacts results, a mid-year discussion is highly likely which could lead to a personal development plan (PDP), signaling the appropriate time to update your resume (Chapter 2). Development feedback from others is instrumental, but patience with yourself must be first and foremost. Career progression does not happen in an instant, hence the terminology of progressive. I have had the privilege and responsibility of mentoring individuals and leading teams. From the range of experience as both the performance reviewer and reviewee, it must be emphasized that unfavorable comments, while difficult to hear, needs to be confronted. Complications will not resolve on their own unless by good fortune a toxic colleague or manager is let go of, or decides to transfer. Be ever mindful of appropriate decorum, especially when comments or strategies veer completely off the rails of rationale.

BEST PRACTICES

1. Many organizations conduct mid and end-of-year reviews. At either, or both points in time, update resumes (Chapter 2) and profiles for consistency in data.
2. Mid-year reflections are often regarded as a box checking exercise. Do not fall into a complacent mindset; evaluate current responsibilities to a preferred career trajectory – consider if anything should be adjusted as to accommodate.
3. When discussing the year ahead, be direct, clear, and open to feedback. What is preferred for the near term may involve a milestone in between. If what you hear is not as expected, pause before responding.
4. In a corporate setting, review sessions are when 'it is about you'– do not allow the opportunity to pass without a performance 'health check' of substance.
5. Rely and lean on facts, not feelings; also, consider tone in messaging.
6. Understand KPIs and the impact on your team, project, or the like.
7. Evaluate expectations for the year ahead– are they realistic (achievable) and relatable (in relationship with broader organizational strategy).
8. Think before you speak; you cannot retract what is said.
9. When in conversation, jot down words, phrases, or topics to research with the help of AI thereafter.
10. Prior to discussing recent achievements and forthcoming goals, reflect on points 6-9 for a few minutes in preparation for candid dialogue.

CONCLUSION

"In literature and in life we ultimately pursue, not conclusions, but beginnings." - Sam Tanenhaus

No two experiences will be the same; each path is as unique as the individual advancing along it. It is important to mention that the corporate landscape is not for everyone. Taking things in stride is essential to sustain the mental gymnastics of engagement and collaboration. The discipline required to maintain expectations is a challenge for most. Johnson (2022, p.57) notes that understanding one's self is an iterative process, and not a singular event. Burnout and deterioration of quality are common when attempting to move too quickly, or commit to tasks that exceed available capacity or a current skill level. The manner a career path is developed, then altered in light of, or in spite of, significant learnings, cannot be expedited. Effective personal growth in progressive.

Companies larger in scale offer a wealth of resources and opportunities for a range of talent and skill sets, often on a global level. The best fit for you will eventually materialize as exposure to various industries and organization sizes occurs. Retracing to Chapter 1, remember that branding is a continuous, purposeful activity, centered on remaining visible (Arruda and Dixson, 2009 p. 58). Strategic brand management is thus no longer a luxury, but a necessity in professional advancement (Vaynerchuck, 2018). People must know who you are, understand what you stand for, and what you are able to accomplish. With the influx of remote and hybrid workplaces, employees new to the corporate scene may find reduced opportunities with chance encounters of those in leadership positions. Adapting to a continuous decline of face-to-face engagement and related visibility is dependent on creativity of intentional interaction.

Maintaining touchpoints is vital. Former mentors, managers, and clients offer a well-rounded network shaping your brand community - those familiar with your persona (Arruda *et al.*, 2009). As future opportunities arise within their separate spheres of influence, you may be a top contender by default as an alliance and trust level already exists. While a role offered may not be a part of a master plan, flexibility and an open mind may introduce a direction not otherwise considered. For better or worse, exposure is key to deciphering how to integrate and capitalize on unique strengths. Over time, evaluate who to engage with, and when the timing to do so is appropriate, as to facilitate continuous growth within the respective industry, division, or profession decided upon. In the end, companies need results to remain viable. Be an individual who is willing and able to develop a plan and see efforts through to completion. Showcase ambition considerate of the bigger organizational picture. Take the first step to guide others towards results, course correct as conditions change, and step back in reflection as moments of success are attained.

APPENDICES

APPENDIX I | KEY CONCEPTS

1 - Personal Brand Development
- Similar in concept to a reputation, a personal brand is representative of the way others perceive you. From this context, consider the value in playing a significant role in distinguishing yourself from peers.
- Identified proficiencies are 'superpowers' – assets in Corporate America.

2 - Resumes 101
- Effective resumes are concise, informative, and relevant to the organization; this structure forming a winning trifecta.
- Just as skill development occurs through exposure, effectively communicating capabilities in written form is a craft that improves from time at task.

3 - Write like a Journalist
- Providing the full picture in correspondence for non-routine, or particularly pressing matters, increases the likelihood that others outside the original audience will be able to associate with the origin of need, and lend additional support to the best of their ability.
- Communicating well does not necessarily mean communicating more.

4 - Stakeholder Management
- Organizational success is dependent upon how well colleagues collaborate.
- Positive associations of the way in which interaction occurs is critical to career advancement; that being the case, where possible, choose your corporate allies wisely.
- When fully present and confident, a person can facilitate dialogue or mediate differences to shape quality relationship management.

5 - Nobody Cares
- The previous call ran over, unaware of the double mute option, software updates not possible to postpone – the plain truth is that simply, nobody cares.
- Business etiquette is a straightforward concept, yet disregarded unconsciously by those who display behavior most in need of change.
- Attention and intention are key principles to understand where conversation is of quality opposed to quantity, and how small adjustments during engagement add up.

6 - Meetings and Conference Calls

- Try to stay calm and speak to what you know. If completely lost for words or an answer, offer a timeframe giving assurance feedback will follow.
- Phrase questions to encourage conversation and collaboration, not to put someone on the spot.
- Accommodating everyone and everything is unrealistic.
- Agendas are instrumental for efficiency; they mustn't be law, but a guide.
- The 'hey while I have you on the line' mention is not a crowd pleaser.
- Familiarity of content, paired with structured outlines, offer the best lines of defense to mitigate wasted time and produce results.

7 – Presentations

- Arriving at an optimal balance of information, tailored to the intended audience, is a lifelong endeavor.
- The wise speak when there is something worth saying, in contrast to a fool who speaks to be heard.
- A quick assessment of what could have gone better isolates areas or techniques to avoid in the next opportunity; conversely, identifying what went well, worth further development for continuous improvement.

8 – Take Action

- It is astonishing to witness the quick nature colleagues and clients come to rely upon those who make it happen.
- Course correction allows incremental movement towards achievement of results.
- From automating reporting to digitally generated meeting notes, AI should no longer be thought of as reserved for the IT department, or engineer minded.

9 - Corporate Environments

- Little in business is coincidental.
- Approach adversaries in a stoic manner and press on.
- Another reality is that companies have a bottom line. When budgetary cuts are required, resources are depersonalized for the sake of the company. You become a number. Regardless of your strengths, contributions, and track record, the cost of business can cost <u>you</u> your job.

10 - Performance Reviews

- A reply that 'increased pay and authority is necessary before performing well' in a role an individual is already being paid for is the wrong answer to the question of why you should be promoted.
- Career progression does not happen in an instant.

- Development feedback from others is instrumental and patience with yourself necessary.

Conclusion
- Strategic brand management is no longer a luxury, but necessary for professional advancement.

APPENDIX II | ACRONYM LIST

While not exhaustive, this list captures frequently used acronyms in corporate settings.

AP	Accounts Payable
AR	Accounts Receivable
B2B	Business to Business
B2C	Business to Consumer
BD	Business Development (Also referred to as Biz Dev)
BPM	Business Process Management
CMS	Content Management System
COB	Close of Business
Corp	Corporate or Corporation
CRM	Customer Relationship Management
CSR	Corporate Social Responsibility
CTA	Call to Action
CV	Curriculum Vitae (Resume outside of the USA)
DOE	Depending on Experience
EOD	End of Day
EMEA	Europe, the Middle East, and Africa
EOW	End of Week
EPS	Earnings Per Share
FTE	Full-Time Employee
HQ	Headquarters
KPI	Key Performance Indicator
MoM	Month over Month
MTD	Month to Date
NDA	Non-Disclosure Agreement
OOO	Out of Office
PDP	Performance Development Plan
PIP	Performance Improvement Plan
P/E	Price to earnings

P&L	Profit and Loss
POC	Point of Contact
PTO	Paid Time Off
QA	Quality Assurance
QC	Quality Control
QBR	Quarterly Business Report
QTR	Quarter
REQ	Requisition
RFP	Request for Proposal
ROI	Return on Investment
SMART	Specific, measurable, attainable, realistic, time-bound (Goal setting)
SMB	Small to Medium Business
SME	Subject Matter Expert
SWOT	Strength, Weaknesses, Opportunities, and Threats (Risk analysis)
WFH	Work from Home
WoW	Week over Week
YTD	Year to Date
YoY	Year over Year

ACKNOWLEDGMENTS

Thank you to family and friends who have and continue to provide unconditional love and encouragement in support of achieving personal and professional goals.

To colleagues I have had the pleasure of working alongside and in collaboration with, I would not be "The Coach" without you.

REFERENCES

INTRODUCTION

Njuguna, C. (2023) '30 inspirational quotes from coaches to spark motivation and drive'. SportsBrief.com. Available at: https://sportsbrief.com/other-sports/38194-30-inspirational-quotes-coaches-spark-motivation-drive/ (Accessed: 14 January 2024).

CHAPTER 1 – PERSONAL BRANDING

Abelli, H. (2021) 'Critical Competencies For Today's Workforce'. Forbes.com. Available at: https://www.forbes.com/sites/forbeshumanresourcescouncil/2021/05/06/10-critical-competencies-for-todays-workforce/?sh=6b0934302273 (Accessed: 21 April 2024).

Arruda, W (2022) 'Personal Branding and The New World Of Work'. Forbes.com. Available at: https://www.forbes.com/sites/williamarruda/2022/09/18/personal-branding-and-the-new-world-of-work/?sh=75aa7fb177b4 (Accessed: 21 November 2023).

Arruda, W and Dixson, K. (2009) *Career Distinction: Stand Out by Building Your Brand*; 1st ed., New York: Wiley.

Coleman, H. (2010) *Empowering Yourself: The Organizational Game Revealed;* 2nd ed. Bloomington, IN: AuthorHouse.

Covey, F. (2020) *The 7 Habits of Highly Effective People.* Simon & Schuster.
April 2020 ed., New York: Simon & Schuster.

Ford, M. (2021) Rule of the Robots: How Artificial Intelligence Will Transform Everything, 1st ed., New York NY: Basic Books.

ManpowerGroup (2023) "From C-Suite to Digital Suite: How to Lead Through Digital Transformation", Manpower Group. Available at: file:///C:/Users/nfron/Downloads/from-c-suite-to-digital-suite-how-to-lead-through-digital-transformation%20(1).pdf (Accessed: 21 November 2023).

Monarth, H. (2022) 'What's the Point of a Personal Brand?'. Harvard Business Review. Available at: https://hbr.org/2022/02/whats-the-point-of-a-personal-brand (Accessed: 27 July 2023).

Weiss, J.H. (2018) *Moving Forward in Mid-Career: A Guide to Rebuilding Your Career after Being Fired or Laid Off.* 1st ed. New York: Skyhorse Publishing.

CHAPTER 2 – RESUMES 101

Arruda, W and Dixson, K. (2009) *Career Distinction: Stand Out by Building Your Brand*. 1st ed. New York: Wiley.

Burdick, C. (2017) 'The History of the Resume'. LinkedIn.Com. Available at: https://www.linkedin.com/pulse/resume-today-beyond-cody-burdick (Accessed: 5 November 2023).

Dormehl, L. (2017) *Thinking Machines: The Quest for Artificial Intelligence and Where It's Taking Us Next,* Tarcher and Perigee, Penguin Random House: 1st ed New York NY.

Ford, M (2021) *Rule of the Robots: How Artificial Intelligence Will Transform Everything*, 1st ed., New York NY: Basic Books.

Gannett, A. (2018) "Do Resume Typos Matter? Here's What Hundreds Of LinkedIn Users Say", Fast Company. Available at: https://www.fastcompany.com/40536077/do-resume-typos-matter-heres-what-hundreds-of-linkedin-users-say (Accessed: 17 November 2023).

Grady, K. (2024) 'Redefining Career Success With 9 Workplace Trends in 2024'. Teal HQ Career Paths. Available at: https://www.tealhq.com/post/future-workplace-trends (Accessed: 2 April 2024).

Hackl, C. (2023) *Into the Metaverse: The Essential Guide to the Business Opportunities of the Web3 Era*. 1st ed. Great Britain, London: Bloomsbury Business.

Heath, C. and Starr, K. (2022) *Making Numbers Count: The Art and Science of Communicating Numbers*. 1st ed. New York, NY: Avid Reader Press.

Weiss, J.H. (2018) *Moving Forward in Mid-Career: A Guide to Rebuilding Your Career after Being Fired or Laid Off*. 1st ed. New York: Skyhorse Publishing.

Winnie, T. (2015) 'These Famous Quotes Will Give You Resume Help'. Jobscan.com. Available at: https://www.quoteslyfe.com/quote/The-simpler-you-say-it-the-more-391621. (Accessed 10 January 2024).

CHAPTER 3 – WRITE LIKE A JOURNALIST

Bagadiya, J. (2023) '500+ Social Media Statistics You Must Know in 2023'. Socialpilot.co. Available at: https://www.socialpilot.co/blog/social-media-statistics (Accessed 22: August 2023).

Bashaw, B. (2019) 'We Analyzed How 38 CEOs Send Emails—Here's What We Found', Slab.com. Available at: https://slab.com/blog/how-ceos-email/ (Accessed: 23 August 2023).

Birchard, B. (2021) 'The Science of Strong Business Writing', Harvard Business Review. Available at: https://hbr.org/2021/07/the-science-of-strong-business-writing (Accessed: 10 December 2023).

Block, R. (2016) 'On the Art of Writing: What Did Thomas Jefferson Really Say?'. LinkedIn.Com. Available at: https://www.linkedin.com/pulse/art-writing-what-did-thomas-jefferson-really-say-richard-bloch (Accessed: 22 August 2023).

Bradbury, R. (2012). *Fahrenheit 451.* 60th anniversary edition. New York: Simon & Schuster.

Branson, R. (2012) *Like a Virgin: Secrets They Won't Teach you at Business School.* 1st ed. London, England: The Penguin Group.

Dormehl, L. (2017) *Thinking Machines: The Quest for Artificial Intelligence and Where It's Taking Us Next*, 1st ed. New York NY: Tarcher and Perigee, Penguin Random House.

Haus, M. (2016) 'Are Your Communication Habits Good Enough? Project Management.com. Available at: https://www.projectmanagement.com/blog-post/18979/Are-Your-Communication-Habits-Good-Enough-- Project Management.com (Accessed: 4 December 2023).

Mahalik, P.K. (2010) 'Using the Five W's and One H Approach to Six Sigma', ISixSigma.com. Available at: https://www.isixsigma.com/basics/using-five-ws-and-one-h-approach-six-sigma/, (Accessed: 4 December 2023).

McKloskey, D.N. (2019) *Economical Writing.* 3rd ed., Chicago and London: The University of Chicago Press.

Newman, N. (2023) 'Journalism, media, and technology trends and predictions 2023', Reutersinstitute.com. Available at: https://reutersinstitute.politics.ox.ac.uk/journalism-media-and-technology-trends-and-predictions-2023#header--8 (Accessed: 26 March 2024).

Singh, M. (2022) 'Social media character limits in 2023 (Free Cheat Sheet and tools)'. Sociality.io. Available at: https://sociality.io/blog/social-media-character-limits/ (Accessed: 22 August 2023).

CHAPTER 4 – STAKEHOLDER ENGAGEMENT

Fearn, N. (2024) 'MIT gives AI the power to 'reason like humans' by creating hybrid architecture'. Live Science.com. Available at: https://www.livescience.com/technology/artificial-intelligence/mit-gives-ai-the-power-to-reason-like-humans-by-creating-hybrid-architecture (Accessed: 13 May 2024)

Ford, M (2021) *Rule of the Robots: How Artificial Intelligence Will Transform Everything,* 1st ed., New York NY: Basic Books

Haan, K. (2023) 'Remote Work Statistics and Trends In 2023'. Forbes Advisor. Available at: https://www.forbes.com/advisor/business/remote-work-statistics/ (Accessed: 13 December 2023)

Herman, A. (2021) *Fixed. How to Perfect the Fine Art of Problem-Solving.* 1st ed. New York: Harper Collins.

Kessler, D. (2018) 'A stakeholder through the heart'. velocitypartners.com. Available at: https://velocitypartners.com/resources/a-stakeholder-through-the-heart/ (Accessed: 10 September 2023)

Kujala, J, Sachs, S., Leinonen, H., Heikkinen, A., and Laude, D. (2022) 'Stakeholder Engagement: Past, Present, and Future, Business & Society', Volume 61, Issue 5, May 2022, Pages 1136-1196. Available at: https://doi.org/10.1177/00076503211066595 (Accessed: 11 December 2023)

Madsbjerg, C. (2023) *Look: How to Pay Attention in a Distracted World*. 1st ed. New York; Riverhead Books

Pink, D. (2018) When: The Scientific Secrets of Perfect Timing. 1st ed. New York: Riverhead Books

Project Management Institute (PMI) (2023) 'Pulse of the Profession 2023: Power Skills, Redefining Project Success | 14th Edition. PMI.org. Available at: https://www.pmi.org/-/media/pmi/documents/public/pdf/learning/thought-leadership/pmi-pulse-of-the-profession-2023-report.pdf?rev=df863a1f6e2e48628679c5c2ce96b3d3&sc_lang_temp=en (Accessed: 4 December 2023).

Tasaka, H. (2020) 'Artificial intelligence'. World Economic Forum. Available at: https://www.weforum.org/agenda/2020/10/these-6-skills-cannot-be-replicated-by-artificial-intelligence/ (Accessed: 13 May 2024)

Taubenfeld, E. (2023) 35 Brilliant Albert Einstein Quotes to Inspire You to Greatness, Readers Digest.com. Available at: https://www.rd.com/article/albert-einstein-quotes/ (Accessed: 2 January 2024).

Vogwell, D. (2003) 'Stakeholder management. Paper presented at PMI® Global Congress 2003—EMEA, The Hague, South Holland, The Netherlands. Newtown Square, PA'. Project Management Institute. Available at: https://www.pmi.org/learning/library/stakeholder-management-task-project-success-7736 (Accessed: 25 October 2023).

Welch, J. (2001) *Get better or Get Beaten*; 2nd ed. New York: McGraw-Hill.

CHAPTER 5 – NOBODY CARES

Browning, Robert (1855). Poem. Andrea del Sarto, Lucrezia.

Willink, J. and Babin, L. (2015) *Extreme Ownership: How U.S. Navy SEALs Lead and Win*, 1st ed. New York: St. Martin's Press.

CHAPTER 6 – MEETINGS AND CONFERENCE CALLS

Ferro, JayTwitter (n.d) [@jayferro]. "The three stages of career development: 1. I can't wait until I'm important enough to be included in meetings. 2. I feel so important being in these meetings! 3. I will do anything legal, and several illegal things, to avoid these meetings." Twitter, 19 November 2021.
https://twitter.com/jayferro/status/1461729270238220301

Indeed (N.d) 'How to Properly Set an Agenda for Your Team Meetings'. Available at: https://www.indeed.com/hire/c/info/team-meetings-agenda (Accessed: 16 November 2023).

Lencioni, P. (2012) *The Advantage – Why Organizational Health Trumps Everything Else in Business*. 1st ed. San Francisco: Jossey-Bass, A Wiley Brand.

Mangia, K (2020) *Working From Home: Making the New Normal Work for You*. 1st ed. Hoboken, New Jersey: Wiley.

Puutio, A. (2023) 'If Your Meeting Doesn't Start With A Question, Don't Schedule It', Forbes.com. Available at:
https://www.forbes.com/sites/alexanderpuutio/2023/10/19/if-your-

meeting-doesnt-start-with-a-question-dont-schedule-it/?sh=3c7d6dbd7e5b (Accessed: 9 November 2023).

Tulgan, B. (2020) The Art of Being Indispensable at Work: Win Influence, Beat Overcommitment, and Get the Right Things Done. 1st ed. Boston, MA: Harvard Business Review Press.

Williams, C. (2024) 'Blending AI And Human Wisdom For Meeting Mastery In 2024'. Forbes.com. Available at: https://www.forbes.com/sites/forbesbusinesscouncil/2024/03/19/blending-ai-and-human-wisdom-for-meeting-mastery-in-2024/?sh=246dbb402f85 (Accessed: 22 April 2024).

Zewe, A. (2023) 'Explained: Generative AI. How do powerful generative AI systems like ChatGPT work, and what makes them different from other types of artificial intelligence?'. MIT News. Available at: https://news.mit.edu/2023/explained-generative-ai-1109 (Accessed: 22 April 2024)

CHAPTER 7 – PRESENTATIONS

Baker, C. & Miller, H.L (2023) 'How a Speech Outline Can Help You Persuade Your Audience'. Leaders.com. Available at: https://leaders.com/articles/public-speaking/speech-outline/ (Accessed: 7 October 2023).

Galle, B. (2017) '15 Fear of Public Speaking Statistics'. BradonGaille.com. Available at: https://brandongaille.com/14-fear-public-speaking-statistics/ (Accessed: 27 December 2023).

Gallo, C. (2014) *Talk Like Ted*. 1st ed. New York, NY: St. Martin's Press.

Goleman, D. (2020). *Emotional Intelligence: Why it can matter more than IQ*. 2nd ed. London, UK: Bloomsbury.

Merriam-Webster (n.d.) Glossophobia, noun Glossophobia Definition & Meaning. Available at: https://www.merriam-webster.com/dictionary/glossophobia (Accessed: 7 October 2023).

Riegel, D. G (2019) 'Saying These 2 Words During a Big Presentation Could Damage Your Credibility - Apologizing may just ruin your presentation'. Inc.com. Available at: https://www.inc.com/deborah-grayson-riegel/stop-saying-im-sorry-in-your-presentations-do-this-instead.html (Accessed: 8 October 2023).

Van Edwards, V. (2024) 'Amplify Your Communication Skills with Generative AI', LinkenIn.com, Available at: https://www.linkedin.com/learning/amplify-your-communication-skills-with-generative-ai (Accessed: 26 May 2024).

CHAPTER 8 – TAKE ACTION

Branson, R. (2011) *Business Stripped Bare: Adventures of a Global Entrepreneur*. 1st ed. England: Penguin Books, Ltd.

Haeger, J. (n.d.) "Speed Mentoring, Flash Mentoring, and Mentoring Circles". HealthTech Diversity by Doing. Stanford Education. Available at: speed-flash-mentoring-circles.pdf (stanford.edu). (Accessed: 11 November 2023).

Hall, J. (2023) 'Why Upskilling And Reskilling Are Essential In 2023', Forbes.com. Available at: https://www.forbes.com/sites/johnhall/2023/02/24/why-upskilling-and-reskilling-are-essential-in-2023/?sh=6e2210414088 (Accessed: 25 March 2024).

Heath, C. and Starr, K. (2022) *Making Numbers Count: The Art and Science of Communicating Numbers.* 1st ed. New York, NY: Avid Reader Press.

Herman, A. (2018) *A lesson on looking.* October. Available at: https://www.ted.com/talks/amy_herman_a_lesson_on_looking/transcript (Accessed: 1/2/2024).

Parker, R. (2023) 'High Achievers: Time to Get Comfortable Being Uncomfortable: 3 steps to silence the fear of failure and take action on your biggest goals'. Psychology Today. Available at: https://www.psychologytoday.com/au/blog/neuroscience-in-your-daily-life/202308/high-achievers-time-to-get-comfortable-being (Accessed: 1/2/2024).

Rhoten, R. (2023) "We can choose to see obstacles or we can see opportunities". Ryan Rhoten.com. Available at: https://ryanrhoten.com/abundance-mindset/ (Accessed: 8 November 2023).

Suleyman, M. (2023) *The Coming Wave: Technology, Power, and the 21st Century's Greatest Dilemma*, 1st ed. New York, NY: Crown Publishing Group

Sutton, R. and Rao, H. (2014). *Scaling up Excellence: Getting to More without Settling for Less*, 1st ed. New York: Crown Publishing.

Yiu, T. (2019) 'How Much Analysis Is Too Much? Don't Let Your Productivity and Decision Making Fall Victim To Analysis Paralysis'. Towards Data Science. Available at: https://towardsdatascience.com/how-much-analysis-is-too-much-e1dfc5b37cbb (Accessed: 1 January 2024).

CHAPTER 9 – CORPORATE ENVIRONMENTS

Bossidy and Charan (2002) *Execution: The Discipline of Getting Things Done*. 1st ed. New York: Random House

Lakhani, K. and Ignatius, A. (2023) 'AI Won't Replace Humans — But Humans With AI Will Replace Humans Without AI', Available at: https://hbr.org/2023/08/ai-wont-replace-humans-but-humans-with-ai-will-replace-humans-without-ai (Accessed: 20 April 2024)

Lee, K-F (2018) *AI Superpowers: China, Silicon Valley, and the New World Order*, 1st ed. New York, NY: Harper Business.

Peek S. (2023) 'Management Theory of Stephen Covey'. Business.com. Available at: https://www.business.com/articles/management-theory-of-stephen-covey/ (Accessed: 6 January 2024).

Soojung-Kim Pang, A. (2020) *Shorter: Work Better, Smarter, and Less—Here's How*, 1st ed. New York, NY: Public Affairs.

Sutton, R. and Rao, H. (2014). *Scaling up Excellence: Getting to More without Settling for Less*, 1st ed. New York: Crown Publishing.

CHAPTER 10 – PERFORMANCE REVIEWS

Davis, M. (2021) '72 Self Reflection Quotes to Inspire You for 2021'. Rize.com. Available at: https://rize.io/blog/self-reflection-quotes (Accessed: 7 January 2024).

Miller, S. (2022) 'Average US Pay Increase Projected to Hit 4.6m% in 2023', SHRM Org. Available at: https://www.shrm.org/resourcesandtools/hr-topics/compensation/pages/us-pay-increase-forecast-for-2023.aspx (Accessed: 5 October 2023).

Perman, C. (2023) 'The best way to get a big raise, have the 'salary talk' and other tips for earning more in 2023' CNBC.com. Available at: https://www.cnbc.com/2023/02/16/are-you-getting-a-pay-raise-this-year.html (Accessed: 1 January 2024).

Tomas Laurinavicius, T. and Main, K. (2023) 'Performance Review Template & Examples (2023)' Forbes Advisor. Available at: https://www.forbes.com/advisor/business/performance-review/ (Accessed: 10 December 2023).

CONCLUSION

Arruda, W and Dixson, K. (2009) *Career Distinction: Stand Out by Building Your Brand*. 1st ed. New York: Wiley.

Johnson, W. (2022) *Smart Growth: How to Grow Your People to Grow your Company*; 1st ed. Massachusetts: Harvard Business Review Press.

Tanenhaus, S. (1986) *Literature Unbound*. 1st ed. New York, NY: *Ballantine Books*

Vaynerchuck, G (2018) *Crushing it!: how great entrepreneurs build business and influence-- and how you can, too*. 1st ed. New York, NY: Harper Business, an imprint of HarperCollins Publishers.

INDEX

A
advancement *1, 6, 15, 32, 45, 48, 89, 94, 96, 110, 114, 125, 129, 132*
AI 6, 17, 18, 27, 37, 49, 61, 74, 84, 87, 95, 99, 109, 121, 123, 131, 140, 143, 144, 146
all-hands *14*
audience . *2, 12, 15, 31, 34, 38, 47, 56, 59, 60, 69, 78, 79, 80, 81, 83, 84, 103, 107, 128, 130*

B
benchmark 13, 115
blue chip 110
body language *11, 45, 46, 82*
brainstorming 96
branding *5, 8, 9, 16, 17, 23, 29, 42, 96, 124, 136*
Branson, Richard 37, 98, 139, 144
business upset *43*

C
career path *4, 26, 124*
chatbot *16, 18, 62*
checklist *6*
clients *4, 48, 51, 70, 72, 84, 95, 96, 121, 125, 131*
collaboration 68, 73, 74, 76, 92, 99, 124, 130, 135
communication *2, 3, 33, 38, 40, 78, 85, 117, 144*
conference room 66, 101
Constructive feedback *21, 112*
consultant *10, 11*
contingency planning 27
corporate allies *45, 129*
corrective measures *24, 98*
cost reduction *15, 49*
course correction 94, 98
cover letter 27
Covey, Stephen 14, 100, 136, 146
credibility *12, 15, 23, 36, 45, 52, 69, 81*
C-suite 72, 137

D

data............ *4, 10, 20, 21, 23, 50, 74, 77, 83, 84, 98, 109, 115, 116, 123*
De Vinci, Leonard... *24*
delegate / delegation... *14, 34, 96*
development ... *1, 3, 4, 5, 8, 10, 14, 26, 27, 29, 30, 33, 41, 43, 55, 65, 73, 80, 82, 86, 93, 103, 104, 111, 113, 115, 116, 121, 128, 130, 142*
digital ...*13, 15, 16, 24, 26, 29, 46, 48, 49, 53, 59, 61, 75, 84, 85, 87, 103, 109, 137*

E

etiquette.. *56, 73, 77, 81, 104, 129*
expectations.. *12, 29, 34, 38, 47, 52, 63, 66, 69, 73, 77, 87, 88, 116, 117, 120, 123, 124*
expertise *5, 26, 34, 36, 55, 78, 81, 95, 96, 109*

F

Facebook *35, 153*
Fahrenheit 451 .... *30, 139*
Ferro, Jay... *65, 142*
forecast.. *14, 146*
Fortune 100 .... *90, 153*
Fortune 500 .... *4, 79*

G

General Electric (GE) *46*
Go/No Go... *44, 98*

H

headcount *49, 90*
human resources *104*
hybrid *14, 17, 125, 140*

I

IBM *25*
identity *2, 5, 8, 18*
image *8, 12, 13, 15, 18*
initiative/ initiatives *4, 11, 13, 23, 62, 94, 96, 99, 103, 110, 116*
integrity *12, 13, 18*
interior design *31, 66, 91, 112*
interpersonal skills... *49*
interview.. *12, 24, 25, 27*

J

journalism *5, 37, 140*

K
K-12 60
Key Performance Indicators (KPI) 115, 116, 134

L
leadership *2, 3, 9, 11, 13, 43, 71, 72, 103, 106, 114, 118, 125, 141*

M
Machine learning.. *49*
Markov chain.. 74
meeting *3, 4, 30, 31, 41, 58, 59, 64, 65, 66, 70, 72, 73, 75, 78, 79, 81, 87, 95, 96, 131, 143*
meetings *2, 10, 14, 17, 56, 61, 67, 68, 70, 74, 77, 116, 142*
Metaverse *28, 138*
Microsoft 25
Mies van der Rohe, Ludwig.. *59*

N
network 5, 64, 80, 92, 108, 111, 125

O
optimization.. 109

P
performance.................. 4, 6, 9, 15, 46, 112, 114, 116, 121, 122, 123, 147
Plato 83
PMI *50, 141*
politics... 108, 140
portfolio *10, 24*
product.. 22, 79
productivity.... *5, 22, 32, 46, 51, 54, 56, 60, 64, 79, 89, 97, 100, 105, 110, 115, 120*
program *9, 32, 37, 49, 101, 102*
project.................. *10, 16, 31, 33, 57, 58, 66, 96, 111, 116, 123, 141, 153*
prompt engineering 37
paid time off (PTO)..68, 77, 134
public speaking 2, 79, 82, 86

Q
Quarterly Business Reports (QBR).. *22, 134*

R
recognition *13, 14, 15, 92, 102, 115*
relationship management... *41, 49, 50, 91, 129*

remote *14, 16, 48, 83, 101, 102, 125, 140*
remove barriers *51*
reputations *8, 12*
resolution *9, 24, 69*
resources *9, 14, 37, 92, 93, 94, 96, 99, 104, 109, 110, 116, 124, 131, 140*
resume *3, 4, 12, 19, 20, 21, 22, 24, 25, 26, 27, 28, 29, 121, 137, 138*
return on investment (ROI) *35, 68, 134*
Risk Register 93, 99

S
scalability *15*
service offering *22, 79*
Six Sigma *33, 139*
social media *24, 35*
staff meetings 67
stakeholder *10, 42, 43, 44, 46, 47, 140, 141*
strategic *2, 9, 14, 40, 42, 111, 119*
subject matter experts (SME) 72, 134
SWOT 93, 99, 134

T
talent 21, 104, 124
technology 6, 16, 27, 57, 84, 95, 140
time management *14*
traits *13, 17, 27, 49, 100, 106*
Twain, Mark 89, 98
Twitter 65, 142

U
upper management 72, 109

V
value-add *19*
visibility 8, 15, 47, 52, 75, 103, 125
volunteering *14, 15, 18, 80*

W
Welch, Jack 46, 142
Wi-Fi 48, 64
Willink and Babin 55
Word choice 24, 30
Work From Home 17
workforce 26, 28, 48, 60, 84, 95, 101, 105, 115, 136
workplace 3, 32, 41, 60, 106, 109, 110, 138
workshop *35, 37, 43, 80*

ABOUT THE AUTHOR

Nicole Fronek, known as "The Coach" and CEO of Two Horse Productions LLC, is based in the Black Hills of South Dakota. Roles supporting Fortune 100 firms have included CBRE Group, Chevron, HP, Citigroup, and Marriott International. With two decades of experience in project delivery and client services, she has built her career on a foundation of helping others achieve their goals. Nicole holds a BA in Communications from California State University, Fullerton, and an MSc in Project Management from The University of Liverpool.

www.nicolefronek.com
Facebook.com/nicolefronek
Instagram: @nicolefronek

www.ingramcontent.com/pod-product-compliance
Lightning Source LLC
Chambersburg PA
CBHW030525080526
44586CB00011B/322